LAUNCHING AND CONSOLIDATING UNSTOPPABLE LEARNING

ALEXANDER MCNEECE

Edited by Douglas Fisher and Nancy Frey

Solution Tree | Press
a division of
Solution Tree

555 North Morton Street
Bloomington, IN 47404
800.733.6786 (toll free) / 812.336.7700
FAX: 812.336.7790

email: info@SolutionTree.com
SolutionTree.com

Visit **go.SolutionTree.com/instruction** to download the free reproducibles in this book.

Printed in the United States of America

Library of Congress Cataloging-in-Publication Data

Names: McNeece, Alexander, author. | Fisher, Douglas, 1965- editor. | Frey, Nancy, 1959- editor.
Title: Launching and consolidating unstoppable learning / author: Alexander McNeece, Ph.D. ; editors: Douglas Fisher and Nancy Frey
Description: Bloomington, IN : Solution Tree Press, [2018] | Includes bibliographical references and index.
Identifiers: LCCN 2018017463 | ISBN 9781945349850 (perfect bound : alk. paper)
Subjects: LCSH: Motivation in education--United States. | Academic achievement--United States. | Learning strategies.
Classification: LCC LB1065 .M358 2018 | DDC 370.15/4--dc23 LC record available at https://lccn.loc.gov/2018017463

Solution Tree
Jeffrey C. Jones, CEO
Edmund M. Ackerman, President

Solution Tree Press
President and Publisher: Douglas M. Rife
Editorial Director: Sarah Payne-Mills
Art Director: Rian Anderson
Managing Production Editor: Kendra Slayton
Senior Production Editor: Tonya Maddox Cupp
Senior Editor: Amy Rubenstein
Copy Editor: Ashante K. Thomas
Proofreader: Elisabeth Abrams
Text and Cover Designer: Rian Anderson
Editorial Assistant: Sarah Ludwig

Acknowledgments

I extend deep gratitude to Douglas Fisher and Nancy Frey for allowing me the opportunity to expound on their insightful and important Unstoppable Learning model. It has been an honor to work with them on this project.

I offer deep appreciation for my influential mentor, Anthony Muhammad, who is the reason I wanted to become a school leader. Through his example, guidance, and friendship, I have grown to focus on being a part of the solution.

With sincere thankfulness, I must acknowledge the entire Solution Tree team for the help and support in making this wish come true. This includes many people, but I especially need to thank Amy Rubenstein, Claudia Wheatley, and Douglas Rife.

Finally, to all the teachers I have had the honor to collaborate with, thank you. This includes my wife, mother, father, aunt, and sister. You make a difference every day. Your actions and care change the world. You bring light to the darkness.

Solution Tree Press would like to thank the following reviewers:

Jennifer Evans
Principal
Burnham School
Cicero, Illinois

Tanya Lange
Associate Principal
Hortonville Elementary School and
  Middle School
Hortonville, Wisconsin

Steve Mefford
Facilitator of Curriculum and
  Professional Learning
Urbandale Community School District
Urbandale, Iowa

Brooke Powers
Mathematics Teacher
Beaumont Middle School
Lexington, Kentucky

Brad Randmark
Assistant Principal
Burnham School
Cicero, Illinois

Rich Smith
Educational Consultant
Clovis, California

Visit **go.SolutionTree.com/instruction** to download the free reproducibles in this book.

Table of Contents

About the Editors

 **Douglas Fisher, PhD,** is professor of educational leadership at San Diego State University and a teacher leader at Health Sciences High and Middle College. He teaches courses in instructional improvement and formative assessment. As a classroom teacher, Fisher focuses on English language arts instruction. He was director of professional development for the City Heights Educational Collaborative and also taught English at Hoover High School.

Fisher received an International Reading Association Celebrate Literacy Award for his work on literacy leadership. For his work as codirector of the City Heights Professional Development Schools, Fisher received the Christa McAuliffe Award. He was corecipient of the Farmer Award for excellence in writing from the National Council of Teachers of English (NCTE), as well as the 2014 Exemplary Leader for the Conference on English Leadership, also from NCTE.

Fisher has written numerous articles on reading and literacy, differentiated instruction, and curriculum design. His books include *Teaching Students to Read Like Detectives*, *Checking for Understanding*, *Better Learning Through Structured Teaching*, and *Rigorous Reading*.

He earned a bachelor's degree in communication, a master's degree in public health, an executive master's degree in business, and a doctoral degree in multicultural education. Fisher completed postdoctoral study at the National Association of State Boards of Education focused on standards-based reforms.

 **Nancy Frey, PhD,** is a professor of educational leadership at San Diego State University. She teaches courses on professional development, systems change, and instructional approaches for supporting students with diverse learning needs. Frey also teaches classes at Health Sciences High and Middle College in San Diego. She is a credentialed special educator, reading specialist, and administrator in California.

Before joining the university faculty, Frey was a public school teacher in Florida. She worked at the state level for the Florida Inclusion Network, helping districts design systems for supporting students with disabilities in general education classrooms.

She is the recipient of the 2008 Early Career Achievement Award from the Literacy Research Association and the Christa McAuliffe Award for excellence in teacher education from the American Association of State Colleges and Universities. She was corecipient of the Farmer Award for excellence in writing from the National Council of Teachers of English for the article "Using Graphic Novels, Anime, and the Internet in an Urban High School."

Frey is coauthor of *Text-Dependent Questions*, *Using Data to Focus Instructional Improvement*, and *Text Complexity: Raising Rigor in Reading*. She has written articles for *The Reading Teacher*, *Journal of Adolescent and Adult Literacy*, *English Journal*, *Voices from the Middle*, *Middle School Journal*, *Remedial and Special Education*, and *Educational Leadership*.

To book Douglas Fisher or Nancy Frey for professional development, contact pd@SolutionTree.com.

About the Author

Alexander McNeece, PhD, is director of instructional services and state and federal grants for Garden City School District in Garden City, Michigan. He is a children's book author and was an award-winning principal at Douglas Elementary School. Alexander previously served as a high school football coach, elementary teacher, and middle school English language arts teacher.

Alexander is an active member of the Metro Bureau's Council of Academic Leadership in Michigan, where he has served as a state-level committee liaison. In 2017, with a team of teachers and principals, he presented to the Michigan State Board of Education based on the tremendous early literacy growth the district achieved with the professional learning communities framework. As a consultant, Alexander has worked with districts around the United States and Canada to help close the achievement gap, transform school culture, strengthen the school-improvement process, and develop Unstoppable Learning pedagogy.

He holds bachelor's and master's degrees in curriculum and instruction from Michigan State University. In 2017, Alexander earned a doctor of philosophy in educational leadership from Eastern Michigan University with his dissertation, "Michigan's Quantitative School Culture Inventories and Student Achievement."

To learn more about Alexander's work, visit www.alexandermcneece.com or follow @AlexMcNeece on Twitter.

To book Alexander McNeece for professional development, contact pd@Solution Tree.com.

Foreword

by Douglas Fisher and Nancy Frey

How many times has someone visited a classroom and noticed that some (or all) of the students were not engaged? But how does that visitor, or any person, measure engagement? Often the focus on engagement is behavioral, and students who are looking out the window or fidgeting in their chair are thought of as unengaged. We think that engagement also includes a cognitive dimension, not just a behavioral one. It may be that the student looking out the window is deeply thinking about the rich mathematics task that the teacher has posed to the group and is near a breakthrough. This classroom visitor would never know unless he or she interacted with the student. So, we are very cautious about classroom observation tools that have observers stand in the back of the room examining student behavior. Engagement is much more complex than that.

And engagement is important. In fact, there is strong evidence that engagement precedes learning. Simply said, when students engage, they have a chance of learning more. Who doesn't want to get students to engage? If you do want students to engage, this book is for you.

We say that because Alexander McNeece has taken on two very important topics that increase the likelihood that students will cognitively engage in learning: (1) launching and (2) consolidating. Taken together, educators can use these two constructs in classrooms to facilitate cognitive engagement. And, as McNeece notes, there is a relationship between cognitive, affective, and behavioral engagement. But we'll let you read the book to learn more about those concepts.

For now, we'd like to focus on the two main approaches that comprise this book: (1) launching learning and (2) consolidating learning.

Launching Learning

First, launching learning includes a collection of strategies that hook students into learning. And there are all kinds of different students that need to be hooked into learning. Some of our students are compliant, and they do what the teacher says, even if they really are not learning much. Others are resistant to learning, and their behavior frustrates the adults who try to teach them. And still others are simply not paying attention to know what is going on in the class to see if they might want to learn something. As educators, we don't get to pick the students we teach. We teach them all. And launching learning is the first step in inviting students into the lesson. There are a host of different ways to launch a lesson, but the learning has to be relevant for students. In fact, we often say that the two most important aspects of a teacher's job (which are also almost never in the job description) are:

- Making content interesting
- Developing humane, growth-producing relationships with students

When these two are in place, students are much more likely to engage. When the content is interesting, and they trust the teacher to guide them in their learning, students take risks and focus on their learning. As a reminder, for most students it's easier to be known as the bad kid rather than the kid who doesn't know. For them to put themselves out there, risking mistakes, learning has to be relevant; and they have to trust the learning environment.

Here's an example from our own lives. Not too long ago, we were at an unnamed educational conference. We were excited to hear a specific session. We even got there early, forgoing the long coffee line, to get good seats. The presenter was an excellent speaker. The digital slides were sharp and clear. But there weren't any connections made between the audience and the content. We decided that it wasn't what we expected or needed, so we left. Checking the conference app, we noticed that there was a session nearby that also seemed relevant to our current work, and we traveled to that room. We missed the introduction and the objectives for the session, but it didn't matter because the presenter regularly returned to the session's purpose, reminding us where he was within the flow of the presentation, and he took time to make connections between the attendee's experiences and their work. When the session was over, we realized that we had each taken several pages of notes on our tablets. Obviously, the content was relevant and engaging.

It's not that a "bad" teacher led the first session and a "good" teacher conducted the second. They both had skills and experience. They both knew their content. One just made the learning relevant for us and made connections with us as learners, while the other did not. That's why we suggest that making content relevant or interesting is one of the most important things a teacher can do, and why we think that this should be included in teachers' job descriptions.

Consolidating Learning

The second area that comprises this book is consolidating learning. Like launching learning, this is a critical aspect of the classroom. It's important for educators to motivate students and get them hooked, but educators also need to help students create opportunities to make connections and see relationships between ideas, concepts, and skills. Most often, students consolidate their learning with other students, which is why we are such strong proponents of collaborative learning. When students work together, interacting with each other, using academic language (especially argumentation), they are much more likely to actually remember their learning. It's not just that they have a chance to apply the information, which they do. It's more than that. Tasks that allow students to consolidate learning provide an opportunity to hear the thinking of others and to clarify their own thinking.

What we appreciate about, and think is unique about, this book is that McNeece profiles several types of students and shows how launching and consolidating tasks invite those students into learning; or to use the language introduced earlier, to engage. Yes, there are any number of tools useful in inviting students into learning and for helping them practice and apply their skills, but then some students are left behind and then blamed for not learning when their teachers use the tools too generically. Rather than simply say that learning is differentiated, McNeece shows how to ensure that students commit to their learning, and become engrossed, absorbed, and captivated by the experiences they have in class. We know that you will enjoy visiting the classrooms that McNeece profiles and accessing multiple strategies that we can all apply in our own classrooms and schools. Enjoy!

Introduction

How do educators help all students learn at high levels? By engaging them. I want to help you develop practices that help your students engage meaningfully with what they are learning, so they feel positive about school, are motivated, and can self-regulate. I offer prompts and anecdotes to encourage you, teachers and administrators for grades preK–12 (especially those newer to the profession), to consider what engaging classroom instruction looks like for students with different mindsets and different needs. I deconstruct student engagement's complexity and offer strategies for reaching these students, because engagement is more than just student compliance and attentiveness. Educators can influence and, most importantly, grow a student's engagement.

In the introduction, I will explain this book's underpinning, which is Douglas Fisher and Nancy Frey's (2015) Unstoppable Learning model. I then drill down into the model's concepts of launching and consolidating learning, which is about growing student engagement through transforming what we do in the classroom. I explain what I think are the most common student engagement mindsets, the student engagement mindset continuum, and how educators can best apply what I offer about them. I also warn readers how *not* to apply that information. Finally, before diving into the substantial content, I overview what's in the book.

This Book's Underpinning

Fisher and Frey have been instrumental in helping educators around the world gain the skills to be great teachers. In their book *Unstoppable Learning: Seven Essential Elements to Unleash Student Potential*, Fisher and Frey (2015) describe seven elements of teaching and learning: (1) planning, (2) launching, (3) consolidating, (4) assessing, (5) adapting, (6) managing, and (7) leading. You can see how they relate in figure I.1 (page 2). All these elements are critical parts of the whole. In this book, I assume you have read Fisher and Frey's (2015) *Unstoppable Learning* and dive deeper, describing

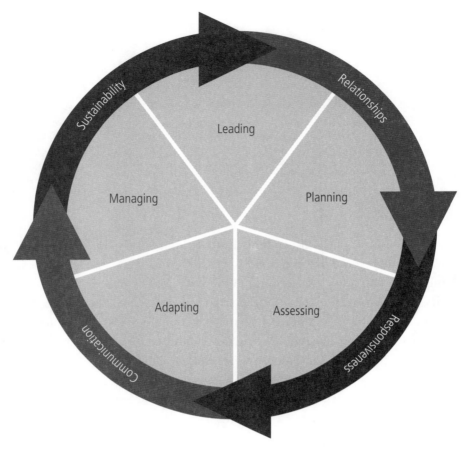

Source: Adapted from Fisher & Frey, 2015.

Figure I.1: Unstoppable Learning systems thinking model.

launching and consolidating in more depth; other books in this series dive into the remaining Unstoppable Learning elements (Hierck & Freese, 2018; Sammons & Smith, 2017; Stinson, 2017; Zapata & Brooks, 2017).

An important component of this model is a systems thinking approach. That approach to teaching and learning is what *Launching and Consolidating Unstoppable Learning* is built on. In a systems thinking approach, all the elements influence the whole concept of Unstoppable Learning. Four overlaying principles bind a systems thinking classroom: (1) relationships, (2) communication, (3) responsiveness, and (4) sustainability.

Relationship building between a teacher and students, and students with each other, is critical. In fact, a close, trusting relationship with a teacher, paired with high-quality instruction from that teacher, improves students' academic and social development (Rimm-Kaufman & Sandilos, n.d.). Learning the proper verbal and nonverbal communication is the next critical principle for all learning's participants, including, of course, teacher and students. Students report that their engagement fluctuates in accordance, partially, with whether teachers communicate with them (Cothran & Ennis, 2000).

Teachers who reflect on students' changing needs are responsive. Educator and author Stephen D. Brookfield (2006) insists that responsiveness is crucial to building trust, which of course, loops back to relationship building. The strategies for each mindset demonstrate responsiveness, since you are responding to each kind of student's particular needs, and that can occur only after you have established a relationship and have communicated with your students. The book's last chapter addresses how to make this engaging instruction sustainable.

The final principle, sustainability, is collaboration. Without the support of a team, classrooms can, through a teacher's hard work, make extraordinary academic gains. The problem with that is that when teachers move on, students lose those academic gains. Additionally, those successes are isolated to those particular classrooms without the ability to share ideas and practices to help all teachers grow.

Fisher and Frey (2015) propose driving questions that help keep educators focused on employing systems thinking. Systems-thinking questions for launching include:

- "What mental models do I use?
- What patterns and changes over time am I noticing?
- What assumptions of my own do I need to challenge?" (p. 174)

Systems-thinking questions for consolidating include:

- "What are the causes and effects of classroom issues I have identified?
- What is the impact of time on these issues?" (p. 175)

I cannot express enough the importance of teachers using the driving questions Fisher and Frey (2015) guide us with. They are the key to reflection and are critical to you when reading this book. Later in the book, I will provide a different mental model for student engagement based on the behaviors that I witnessed as a teacher and principal, and that you can read about in research. The driving questions are there to challenge your assumptions about students and their level of engagement in your classroom. They are there to help you launch the learning in your classroom. Furthermore, the questions for consolidating learning exist to help you critically reflect on what you are doing while you teach. John Hattie (2012) reminds us to "know thy impact." What you do in your classroom is what matters the most. You have the biggest impact on student engagement. Use those systems-thinking questions and the content in this book to help make a great impact.

What It Means to Launch and Consolidate Learning

Launching and consolidating learning are elements of classroom instruction and, when done well, increase student engagement. You can think of both as a dinner metaphor. Launching learning is about preparing for a great meal. Think of when you create a feast for people. How do you invite your guests? What attentive touches do you create? What preparations have you made? Consolidating learning is the meal itself—the thing that guests bite into.

Fisher and Frey's (2015) model separates launching from a lesson's instruction. This is an essential takeaway from the systems thinking model. You cannot succeed without planning for both launching and consolidating, and both exist to engage students in their own distinctive ways. Launching is the context you create for the learning, and consolidating is the work you structure with which students will learn.

Fisher and Frey (2015) open the launching section of their book with a story of student anxiety about school. Let me be clear—the anxiety is about school, not learning. A low-engagement class or school format and structure—not learning itself—create anxiety. I have some personal experience with this as a parent. My daughter experienced severe anxiety in seventh grade. She had an advanced mathematics teacher that she, despite trying to, couldn't connect with. Her feelings manifested into severe physical symptoms around the tests in that class. Even though she had a near perfect grade, the anxiety overwhelmed her. We had never experienced this and didn't know the cause. She missed two months of school while we visited all the best doctors in the area. In the end, two things re-engaged her in school: the volleyball team and a different mathematics teacher. If switching teachers isn't possible, supporting that teacher so he or she can learn how to positively engage students is critical.

What Does It Mean to Launch Learning?

Launching learning is how teachers introduce content in the classroom. It "marks [students'] entry point" (Fisher & Frey, 2015, p. 8). Urgently scrutinizing our education practices (Holmes, 2012) helps us better reach students. Fisher and Frey's (2015) driving questions about this aspect of instruction promote that scrutiny: "What are my instructional goals for students? Where are opportunities to make learning relevant? What misconceptions and errors do I anticipate? How can I invite students into learning? What expert thinking do my students need to witness?" (p. 174).

Use these questions when you are planning to launch the learning in your classroom. You'll see in each chapter that I paid special attention to each of these questions in the teacher A and teacher B scenarios.

What Does It Mean to Consolidate Learning?

If launching learning is like setting the table, consolidating learning is the meal itself. Not every guest will eat every part of the meal, but each guest has a favorite. Consolidating learning is about what teachers do with their instructional time. The Unstoppable Learning model compels teachers to ask themselves the following driving questions about this aspect of instruction (Fisher & Frey, 2015): "How can I structure learning tasks to ensure complexity? How can I structure learning tasks to facilitate interaction? How can I design learning tasks to foster independence?" (p. 175).

These questions are the crux of developing lessons that will help students build competence through thinking through complex concepts, support each other through collaborative classroom activities, and find a level of independence in their learning. Each of the chapters on the student engagement mindsets takes these questions into account when looking at the instructional strategies. Finally, I wrote this book assuming you have read Fisher and Frey's (2015) *Unstoppable Learning*. The mindsets are the frame around launching and consolidating learning. If you launch and consolidate in your classroom, using the student engagement mindsets to complement this work, you can engage students with different needs.

Student Engagement Mindsets

There are five mindsets. You may be tempted to silently label students instead of identifying mindsets and using them to guide your instruction. Reframe your thoughts if you catch yourself thinking, "That student is an agitator" or something similar. This contributes to bias, which can negatively affect students who are struggling (Friedrich, Flunger, Nagengast, Jonkmann, & Trautwein, 2015). Watch for and work against bias in yourself.

- **Agitator mindset:** Students with this mindset are at the far-left end of the engagement continuum (see figure I.2 on page 8). They are less engaged than their classmates. Students with the agitator mindset actively work against the teacher, are overtly disruptive, and chronically underperform.

- **Retreater mindset:** Students with this mindset are withdrawn. They don't attempt work, but they do not disrupt others. They also chronically underperform.

- **Probationer mindset:** Students with this mindset do their work only when outside forces compel them. They never complete high-quality work. They work to avoid punishment.

- **Aficionado mindset:** These high-achieving students think of school as a game, and they play it well. They do exceptionally well. Extrinsic motivators (like earning high grades, making a positive impression, and winning awards) drive them to complete work and achieve accolades. Most educators identify with this mindset, so pay attention to whether you're seeing through that lens as you read.

- **Academician mindset:** Students with this mindset sometimes have enough knowledge to teach content. They have an internal drive for learning in that content area, and it shows in their behaviors. They fully engage in learning and sometimes move beyond extrinsic motivators like grades or awards. Learning is their primary interest.

These are the roles our students play based on their engagement. Each mindset benefits from specific tactics to increase or keep motivation. Using those tactics can help you move students up the student engagement mindset continuum.

How Not to Apply the Mindsets

Many teachers think they see students with the aficionado and academician mindsets in honors classes; they think they see students with probationer and retreater mindsets in remedial classes; they think they see those with agitator mindsets in detention or suspension. This thinking is an oversimplification. Thinking this way gives educators results like spotty engagement and inconsistent student success. Let us recognize that our current approach might be *creating* or *reinforcing* the harmful student engagement mindsets.

Furthermore, separating students into different classes (*tracking*) or classroom groups (*ability grouping*) based on their engagement mindsets is not the best option.

- **Separating and grouping students threatens to increase bias:** A Brown Center on Education Policy at Brookings (Loveless, 2013) report warns that "grouping students by ability, no matter how it is done, will inevitably separate students by characteristics that are correlated statistically with measures of ability, including race, ethnicity, native language, and class" (page 15). Groups like these already struggle in the classroom under the weight of bias (National Center for Education Statistics [NCES], 2002).

- **Tracking and grouping have negligible, and sometimes detrimental, effects:** Research shows (Betts & Shkolnik, 2000; Lleras & Rangel, 2009), for instance, those "lower grouped for reading instruction learn substantially less, and higher-grouped students learn slightly more over the first few years of school, compared to students who are in classrooms that do not practice grouping" (Lleras & Rangel, 2009, p. 279).

Remember: the mindsets exist to guide instruction—not to pigeonhole students or enable misperceptions about their abilities. Some kids are in crisis, but it's up to teachers to engage them.

The Student Engagement Mindset Continuum

Student engagement is a continuum from disengaged to highly engaged. Students can move either direction on that continuum depending on what they experience and choose. It can vary from subject to subject and teacher to teacher (Darr, 2012). There are common threads in the research on student engagement. For example, psychology professors' Richard M. Ryan and Edward L. Deci's (2000a, 2000b) self-determination theory shows how students move from unmotivated to intrinsic motivation. Education researcher Phil Schlechty's (2001) engagement framework highlights the behavioral manifestations of engagement, moving from rebellious to authentic. Finally, education professors Sitwad Saeed and David Zyngier's (2012) complex model blends Ryan and Deci's (2000a, 2000b) motivation work and Schlechty's (2001) engagement framework to explain student engagement behavior and the motivation underneath. I have combined all this research with my own teaching experiences to develop specific engagement mindsets and put them into a continuum of disengaged to engaged.

As I begin describing student mindsets, it is important to remember three points.

1. These mindsets evolved from the existing body of social scientific research (Saeed & Zyngier, 2012; Schlechty, 2001). They are rooted in hard work researchers have done and published. Without their hard work, the student engagement mindsets would not exist.

2. My experiences as a student, teacher, principal, and parent drove my thinking when developing these mindsets.

3. The mindsets are only that. They are *not* actual students, and they are not labels for students. Students change behavior from class to class and day to day. I don't condone labeling students. We are labeling *behavior* to identify positive and negative consequences. This student engagement model exists only to assist educators to help students grow.

Figure I.2 (page 8) shows the student engagement mindset continuum. Let me first explain it; then I will call attention to how important it is to address students with the agitator mindset and the retreater mindset. You can see, from left to right, the mindsets that are least to most engaged. The zone of critical need highlights those mindsets of students who need immediate attention—agitator and retreater. You can also see which possess the fixed and growth mindsets, which I'll discuss further throughout the book and specifically in chapter 2 (page 27).

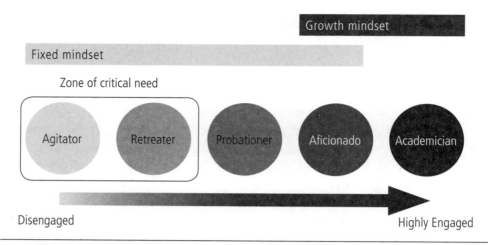

Figure I.2: Student engagement mindset continuum.

Special Attention for Agitator and Retreater Mindsets

The continuum points out the zone of critical need. Those with the agitator and retreater mindsets need immediate attention. These students are at the highest risk of dropout or academic failure in your school, the dangers of which are highlighted in chapter 2 (page 27). Note that students who underperform are capable of more than they're accomplishing. The continuum indicates mindsets only—not potential. Sadly, these students in the zone of critical need will experience disciplinary problems, attendance issues, and social issues with other students and teachers (Appleton, Christenson, & Furlong, 2008). Unfortunately, the education system has few solutions for these students. Many times, they are suspended or fail out of school. Some districts have created alternative schools or programs. In the best cases, these placements offer alternative methods, like those in the How to Reach Them sections of this book. These students needn't be trapped in their current mindsets in a class that is intentionally less rigorous without complex work that exhibits their competency.

When devising ways to help students with the agitator or retreater mindset, educators must consider multiple factors. First, students need academic challenge. Sometimes rigor is swapped for compliance (Sedlak, Wheeler, Pullin, & Cusick, 1986, as cited in Schussler, 2009). Districts cannot put the least experienced or least capable teachers with our most challenging populations. Alternative programs for students with the agitator and retreater mindsets need the best teachers.

Next, lack of academic challenge in the classroom communicates disrespect to a young mind. Research shows that students actually want academic challenges (Sizer & Sizer, 1999). Students with the agitator and retreater mindsets perceive short-term gains when they avoid work. They ultimately feel that the teachers don't care enough to try. When a student has a bargain-making teacher, one who barters away school rules or learning norms for behavioral compliance, that student gets a crushing blow to engagement (Schussler, 2009). Alternative program teachers who work with students who underperform must scaffold instruction and make it more complex gradually. These students need missions (highly complex and highly engaging activities) more than students with any other mindset.

My wife was an alternative high school teacher in Michigan. Her school has helped many students succeed with its intense level of care and instructional expertise. Imagine being a disengaged student who transfers to a place where all the adults communicate and work to make sure you succeed. It creates a relatedness and a positive affective bond. My wife's former students still seek her out and thank her. When the instruction matches the student-teacher bond, the student is more likely to take risks and leave the retreater or agitator mindset behind (Parsons, Nuland, & Parsons, 2014).

It is important to recognize that not all students begin with an agitator or retreater mindset and then move forward on the continuum; some come to us already with the probationer, aficionado, and academician mindsets. In this book, I focus on ways to help students move forward on the continuum from wherever they are and help academician mindsets maintain the highest level of engagement.

What's in This Book

Chapter 1 will define student engagement in regard to the five mindsets on student engagement, link it to Ryan and Deci's (2009) self-determination theory (SDT; which asserts that autonomy, competence, and relatedness are crucial to engagement), and further clarify its importance. This chapter will also take into consideration student perception in order to understand how students perceive assigned tasks. You'll see terms like *chores*, *games*, *burdens*, and *missions* throughout to that end.

Chapters 2 through 6 will cover each of the five mindsets on the student engagement mindset continuum: (1) agitator, (2) retreater, (3) probationer, (4) aficionado, and (5) academician. No matter what a student's grade level, all learners need to feel a high level of relatedness, competence, and autonomy. Each chapter will tie those concepts together and explain how a teacher can use them to engage students. For each, I identify those students' motivations. These chapters open with a description of an actual student I taught or coached who had the specific mindset, and I describe the mindset in detail. Then, the launching and consolidating sections are balanced. The launching sections present classroom scenarios that highlight strong hooks, and the consolidating sections present a critical concept or multiple research-validated strategies when engaging students with that mindset. Chapter 7 offers guidelines to help you, preK–12 teachers and administrators, create a culture of engagement throughout your school, increasing sustainability.

What you read in the coming chapters helps you build the systems thinking instructional principles—(1) relationships, (2) communication, (3) responsiveness, and (4) sustainability—you need to engage students. Let's dive in.

CHAPTER 1

STUDENT ENGAGEMENT

Teacher instruction either inspires or dulls engagement. The launching (contexts) and consolidating (situations) that you create influence students more than any other aspect of their education (Parsons et al., 2014). Other elements can inspire students, but your teaching practices are at the center of a student's desire to learn in your classroom. Sadly, educators often focus improvement initiatives on changing students, not changing their own practices. I, too, have been guilty of this. All the research in this book (including Dweck, 2006; Fisher & Frey, 2015; Muhammad, 2018; Ryan & Deci, 2000a, 2000b) tells us that educators are the ones who need to adjust. It also tells us that when we *do* adjust and use the most effective strategies, our students are more likely to succeed (Hattie, 2012).

How should educators and other stakeholders define engagement? What is its significance? How can they measure it? What are its elements? How can educators and stakeholders implement those elements? We'll answer these questions in this chapter.

Definition

Because I reveal what the motivations are for each mindset, let me distinguish between the two concepts. Although some use these terms interchangeably, *motivation* is not equivalent to *engagement*. *Motivation* prompts us to act; it's the driving force behind what we educators do. Ryan and Deci (2000a) distinguish between two main types—(1) intrinsic and (2) extrinsic. Intrinsic motivation means "doing something because it is inherently interesting or enjoyable" and extrinsic motivation means "doing something because it leads to a separable outcome" (Ryan & Deci, 2000a, p. 55). Motivation that's intrinsic comes from within; extrinsic comes from elsewhere, and the most common in traditional classrooms are rewards (a free homework pass, for example) and punishments (a docked grade for incomplete homework).

Engagement is bigger than that. It blends positive motivation with academics, feelings about school, and self-regulating behaviors. It may help to think of the relationship like this: engagement is the destination, instruction is the car, and motivation is the gasoline.

If asked about engagement, most teachers would identify elements of student behavior like raising hands, attending class, or completing homework. When a student is disengaged, it may be easy to identify behaviors such as sleeping, doing other work, or even disrupting as disengagement. In my experience, when teachers talk about engagement, we identify behavior first because it's observable. As researchers and education consultants Adena M. Klem and James P. Connell (2004) spell out, "Regardless of the definition, research links higher levels of engagement in school with improved performance" (page 3). That bare-bones breakdown implies how significant engagement is.

Significance

Student engagement is a valuable tool for predicting academic performance. In fact, it is a "robust predictor of student learning, grades, achievement, test scores, retention, and graduation" (Skinner & Pitzer, 2012, p. 21), as student disengagement can lead to dropping out. Increasing student engagement helps educators to change the school, district, community, and, most important, a student's life. To help elaborate on this point, I need to share a personal story.

I was a Detroit kid. Living three doors down from me was my best friend for most of my childhood, Joshua. We spent every day together for most of our young lives. Joshua and I both attended public school until ninth grade. At that point, we began attending different schools. I knew Joshua was a brilliant, intellectual guy—he was an avid science, fantasy, historical fiction, and comic book reader and had deep passions for the arts, including anime (long before it was popular in the U.S.) and all kinds of music from all over the world. He excelled at social studies and science. Beyond that, he was a kind and moral person; he was the voice of reason when we were heading toward neighborhood trouble.

Joshua dropped out of high school at sixteen. Students who drop out are less likely to find jobs, less likely to earn a living wage, more likely to live in poverty, and more likely to suffer from a variety of adverse health outcomes (Rumberger, 2011). They're also more likely to commit crimes (Levin, Belfield, Muennig, & Rouse, 2007).

Joshua experienced many of the life events the statistics say a dropout has. He had a daughter when he was still getting his life together. I have thought about his daughter, whom he named after me and who is my goddaughter, and how life has also stacked the deck against her. According to professors Clive R. Belfield, Henry

M. Levin, and Rachel Rosen (2012), and Schuyler Center for Analysis and Advocacy (2008), children born to parents who didn't complete high school are more likely to drop out, too. Despite those statistics, I do have good news, which I'll share at the end of the book (page 93).

While reflecting on his education, Joshua doesn't mince words:

> My teachers would let the good students do nothing. I was polite and thoughtful; they never pushed me for work or to think. As long as I was quiet, I was doing my job. After a time, I could just stay home and get the same thing done (J. Smith, personal communication, August 16, 2018).

How does a student wind up on this path? Later in the book, I'll introduce you to one of the student engagement mindsets that Joshua represents—the retreater (page 37). This is why you and I are here: to make sure students like my best friend don't get left behind.

Elements

Engagement is essential to your students' success. Teachers are empowered when they understand the following engagement models and can leverage those elements to influence greater engagement in their classrooms and schools.

I include two plentiful, interconnected engagement elements.

1. Cognitive, affective, and behavioral model:

    • Cognitive

    • Affective

    • Behavioral

2. Self-determination theory:

    • Autonomy

    • Competence

    • Relatedness

Those interconnections center on thinking, emotions, and independence, all of which lead to students' choices about whether to engage in school.

Student Engagement Trifecta: Cognitive, Affective, and Behavioral

Engagement appears in three dimensions: (1) affective (feelings), (2) behavioral, and (3) cognitive (adapted from Fredricks, Blumenfeld, & Paris, 2004; Guthrie & Wigfield, 2000; Parsons et al., 2014). Figure 1.1 (page 14) is a graphic representation of this concept, showing how the dimensions relate.

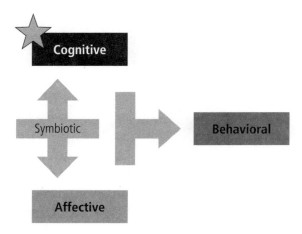

Source: Adapted from Appleton et al., 2008; Parsons et al., 2014.

Figure 1.1: Student engagement model.

The first two elements of the student engagement model—cognitive and affective—are symbiotic. They either strengthen or dissolve in unison. The behavioral dimension relies on those two.

Cognitive

Cognition initiates engagement. This is the student's structure, interaction level, and thinking. Imagine a classroom without a teacher. This classroom would lack any cognitive engagement with learning. Now imagine a classroom with a teacher who only lectures. Those students would have varied cognitive engagement levels. Some students would listen and think, while others would not. Finally, imagine a classroom where the teacher structures the learning in multiple levels of listening, including collaboration with teacher and peers. It also would include independent thinking, critical thinking, talking, game playing, and other instructional frameworks. That teacher would maximize the possibility of cognitive engagement.

Cognitive engagement is also the student's willingness to try to understand the content (Rimm-Kaufman, Baroody, Larsen, Curby, & Abry, 2015). Going back to the lecture example, some students would make an effort to listen and learn, while others would zone out. Additionally, the classroom that had mixed methods would have increased student willingness and higher learning levels (Grant, Lapp, Fisher, Johnson, & Frey, 2012; Young, 2017). The star in figure 1.1 makes it clear that, because educators control the learning methods and structures, cognition is the most important element. In most traditional classrooms, we determine what content we expose a student to and how we present it. Teachers don't directly control how students feel about the school, but the cognitive experiences they offer culminate in students' feelings about school. Students work harder, enjoy learning, and share ideas more freely in classes when the teacher shows warmth, caring, and individual responsiveness (Rimm-Kaufman et al., 2015).

Affective

The affective dimension is how a student feels about school and how connected he or she feels to the school and classroom. Students need positive relationships to the school at large, as well as to their teachers (as explained earlier), the content (see Self-Determination Theory: Autonomy, Competence, and Relatedness, page 16), and each other (Brown & Larson, 2009), and these relationships are intertwined. Belonging is such an important need that loneliness can compromise cognition (Cacioppo & Hawkley, 2009). A positive relationship to academics doesn't ordinarily follow social struggles. Education professor Deborah Schussler (2009) states, "Students who do not feel that they belong on the football field or in the student council also feel that they do not belong in the classroom" (p. 117).

Behavioral

Student behavior, positive and negative, is a manifestation of the cognitive and affective dimensions. When students experience sustained issues in cognitive or affective engagement, they are far more likely to develop issues in behavior (Cairns & Cairns, 1994; Estell, Farmer, & Cairns, 2007, as cited in Farmer et al., 2011). A student may have routinely disengaged in another class led by other teachers, but if you can structure the classroom to hook their interest with fun methods—all the while building a positive relationship—that student will engage. Have you ever wondered why the same teachers, year in and year out, produce high levels of learning? In my experience, these teachers operate the way I just described.

Focusing on student behavior to improve student engagement is akin to treating the pain for an earache—you're treating a symptom, not the cause. It's the easiest way to gauge engagement because it is observable. You increase feelings of connection when you launch and consolidate learning—with its systems thinking focus on relationships, communication, responsiveness, and sustainability. Those feelings can help students connect even further with the lessons you provide. The cognitive and affective dimensions work together to help students self-regulate, which improves behavior. This creates an upward spiral of positive classroom experiences where success reinforces success. Behavior is evidence of what the cognitive and affective components produce between them.

A concept outlined in Ryan and Deci's (2009) self-determination theory can help underscore this phenomenon, where good instruction increases affect toward school and changes student behavior.

Self-Determination Theory: Autonomy, Competence, and Relatedness

We have needs: to feel involved in something that matters to us, to feel capable, and to belong. For example, when I was a teacher, I felt compelled to have next week's lesson plans done the Friday before I left school; I wanted to feel involved in something that matters to me. When you write a paper for your doctoral-level class, you put in the effort and do not expect negative feedback; you want to feel capable. And losing a friend is hard; you want to belong. SDT, simplified here for ease, explains these desires. SDT states that all humans seek three things: (1) autonomy, (2) competence, and (3) relatedness, whose interrelatedness appears in figure 1.2. That applies in the classroom too.

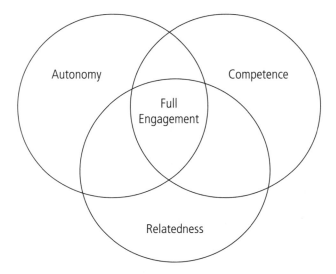

Source: Adapted from Ryan & Deci, 2009.

Figure 1.2: Venn diagram for autonomy, competence, and relatedness.

And so, if launching learning is about creating a positive environment (and beginning to build positive relatedness toward the content), consolidating learning is about building a situation for students that allows autonomy and competence all students need before they can engage. There are also relatedness elements to any consolidating lesson, because this should also be a highly collaborative structure.

Collaborative structures do build relatedness, but they also support both the autonomy of a lesson and give necessary supports for students to gain competence. They are very important. In this book, I try to include these elements to engage you as readers. You'll see those efforts in the presence of multiple strategy choices—you have the autonomy to choose which appeal to you. You will feel competent when I highlight a strategy that you know is a strength in your classroom or when you recognize a student engagement mindset and have antidotes of your own that work with them. I also share personal anecdotes and direct questions to establish a positive relationship between us.

The following sections discuss autonomy, competence, and relatedness in turn. In later chapters, as you read about the student engagement mindsets, I'll describe a specific recipe of autonomy, competence, and relatedness that each mindset needs most.

Autonomy

Essentially, we all want control over what we do and where we go. That is autonomy. Our brains are hardwired to achieve this (Deci & Ryan, 2014). Every person experiences this feeling. Parents may easily see this in their child's stages, from toddlerhood to teenagehood—insisting on dressing oneself despite a long process and resulting eclectic ensemble, to audibly resisting a curfew.

As young people, students crave this same independence. However, much of the traditional education process is scripted. The teacher has roles. The students have roles. Flipping that approach to allow students to take the teacher role can help increase autonomy. I know a mathematics interventionist who does this. Her students come with identified skill gaps, and usually they have been sitting quietly during that topic. They appear withdrawn and disengaged. When they work with the interventionist who, during small-group lessons, has *students* lead games with each other, the interventionist reports that the students love it and do not consider it a burden (T. Remington, personal communication, August 16, 2018).

How do teachers in your school allow autonomy? Do you consult with students to see what topics interest them most and how they want to learn about them? In *Better Learning Through Structured Teaching*, Fisher and Frey (2008) guide educators to student autonomy: a gradual release of responsibility. See table 1.1.

Table 1.1: Gradual Release of Responsibility

Teacher Responsibility	Student Responsibility
Explicit instruction	"I do it."
Guided instruction	"We do it."
Collaboration	"You do it together."
Independence	"You do it alone."

Source: Fisher & Frey, 2008.

This is the type of instruction that should occur in every classroom every day. The gradual release of responsibility gives a student the structured autonomy for his or her own learning. Student responsibility for learning increases as teacher responsibility for instruction decreases. A teacher assumes the most responsibility when giving explicit instruction, ensuring student understanding of what they are about to learn and why (Fisher, 2008). Then, students and the teacher work together on the learning during guided instruction. This gives the teacher a chance to both model thinking and gauge student comprehension via prompting, facilitating, questioning, or leading tasks that increase comprehension (Fisher, 2008). The next shift in responsibility moves students to collaborative work with peers, where they use problem solving, discussion, and negotiation (Fisher, 2008). They have a chance to play with ideas, take risks, and teach and learn from each other. Autonomy, competence, and relatedness are strong components of this step. Finally, students receive a chance to independently apply what they learn. A major misconception is that this final layer is the assessment; it is not. Students must have individual practice before a teacher does a final assessment.

Decreasing the teacher's responsibility creates more opportunities for him or her to work with individual students and small groups, allowing for daily formative assessment and feedback. The most effective teaching strategies to improve student achievement, as researcher and professor John Hattie (2012) notes—classroom discussions, clarity, reciprocal teaching, positive formative assessment, cognitive task analysis, self-questioning, and self-reporting grades—can only occur in a gradual release of responsibility format.

It is important to note that this is not a linear shifting of responsibility, but the model's message is clear: scaffold students toward independence through guided instruction and peer collaboration. The gradual release of responsibility is a way to conceptualize consolidating learning.

Do you see the gradual release of responsibility in your instruction? Do you intentionally build its elements into your lesson plans? If you could add one step to your class tomorrow, which would it be and how would you accomplish it?

Competence

We are creatures of habit for a reason; routines are safe and outcomes are predictable. We feel successful, which adds to the sense that we are capable, or competent. We develop prototypes and schemas for how the world works, and we work to master that system. Cognitive psychologists Jean Piaget (1926) and Eleanor Rosch (1973) conceived of the concepts of prototypes and schemas for how the world works, and Ryan and Deci (2009) claim that we work to master those prototypes and schemas. In *Drive*, author Daniel H. Pink (2009) labels this phenomenon *mastery*. Pink (2009) points out the irony—that mastery is entirely elusive. There is always a deeper level to obtain. We push through frustration in hopes of achieving the excitement of mastering a concept or skill, but it is mastery that drives us to do that. Competence enables higher-level performance and risk taking that beget greater levels of success (Pink, 2009).

What happens when we don't feel competent? Often, we'll disengage. Disengagement is strongly associated with a student's beliefs about his or her academic ability (Patrick, Skinner, & Connell, 1993, as cited in Legault, Green-Demers, & Pelletier, 2006). Students cannot begin a complex task if they believe they lack competence, even though they may have the skills to begin the work (Deed, 2008b). When the student sees the learning as a mountain, he or she would rather walk around the mountain than face the perceived insurmountable challenges of the climb. Feeling competent means students are more likely to seek further development in an area. Moreover, students' level of perceived competence is a better predictor of performance than their actual ability (Pajares & Schunk, 2002).

Do your students feel competent in the subject that you teach? How do you enable that feeling in students, and how can you tell when they feel it?

We move to self-determination theory's relatedness element next.

Relatedness

The ancient Greek philosopher Aristotle said that humans are social animals. We seek connections with others. We want to feel valued. Young people, in particular, come with a strong desire to please adults (Durden, 2011), though they also seek it with peers. And this goes beyond abstract notions. Teachers who emotionally support students report higher cognitive, emotional, and social engagement in their students (Rimm-Kaufman et al., 2015). Relatedness with your students is the most important job of a teacher. Author Maya Angelou's (2002) experience demonstrates this importance. She became selectively mute for a number of years after a man she testified against was killed following his release from police custody. It was not until a teacher connected with her did she choose to use her voice.

For students to develop a sincere connection to school, they "need frequent, affectively pleasant or positive interactions with the same individuals, and they need these interactions to occur in a framework of long-term, stable caring and concern" (Baumeister & Leary, 1995, p. 520). Interpersonal methods build trust, and trust is crucial to relatedness. Psychological scientist Jeanne E. Ormrod (2003) says such teachers "are warm, caring individuals who, through a variety of statements and actions, communicate a respect for their students, an acceptance of them as they are, and a genuine concern about their well-being" (p. 482). How does a teacher build this connection? Make sure that instructional methods include daily guided instruction and collaboration activities. They slowly help students engage with each other and with you, the teacher. When students and teachers are working together, it changes the interactions and eventual relationships for all of them.

Do your students feel relatedness with you? How about with their peers in your classroom? How do you encourage trust and collaboration?

Student Perception

Based on my experience, students will approach tasks or the work you structure in your class different ways depending on their engagement level and the lesson's complexity. The rubric in figure 1.3 reveals how students view any one lesson.

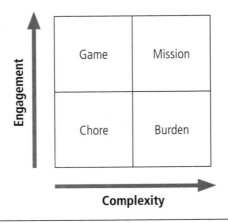

Figure 1.3: Engagement and complexity rubric.

Lessons can feel like chores, games, burdens, or missions. I developed this model using a simple construct of engagement on the left *y*-axis, beginning low and moving up to high, and the *x*-axis beginning with low complexity on the left. This rubric should help you frame classroom work as you move through the next chapters. I'll use these terms to help explain student perceptions of classroom experiences. The aim is to develop high-complexity, high-engagement experiences, but it is important to recognize and be able to describe the experience when we are not reaching that goal.

Chore: Low Complexity, Low Engagement

Does your child—the one at home—like to take out the garbage? When he or she does take it out, does he or she align the cans neatly at the street, with all rubbish ready for an efficient pick up? When my son takes out the garbage, his engagement is minimal at best. There is always something else attracting his attention, and his disengagement with the chore reveals itself as needing to be reminded several times to get it done.

Chores are low-complexity, low-engagement tasks—something students feel they must get through. What do your students consider a chore? Are there small tasks they must do, such as doing traditional bell work or copying their agenda into a planner? Chances are, your students treat them the way they treat their chores at home, and you may use rewards to get them to complete these tasks. They may complete them to avoid punishment.

Game: Low Complexity, High Engagement

Does anyone have to force you to play your favorite game or app? Of course not! Most games and game-like apps like *Candy Crush Saga* and *Angry Birds* are low complexity, high-engagement tasks, and they employ specific tactics to draw you in. They are usually sleek and visually appealing. You determine when and for how long you play it. It's social, creating different, positive connections between you and your friends. It provides different levels of challenge, each of which players must master before moving to the next. Those elements, wrapped up in a simple, routine task, release hormones in the brain that make us feel good (Dockterman, 2013; Migala, 2015).

Teachers try to replicate some of these elements—for instance, presenting a small task and providing extrinsic motivation (rewards) to raise student interest or compulsion. Think of the holiday-themed spelling list or acrostic poem. Recall the scene from *Dead Poets Society* (Haft, Henderson, Witt, Thomas, & Weir, 1989) where the teacher has students repeat short lines from canonized literature while kicking a ball. The boys enjoy kicking the ball and repeating the lines loudly, but there is no analysis. They are not asked to consider the literature or their relationship to the students, curriculum, or critical thinking, but they come to understand being able to repeat information has little consequence. These low-complexity tasks are an attempt to engage students. Authentic minor tasks—those that connect with student interests—can be an important scaffolding technique to build a specific skill, but a classroom cannot provide only games. Otherwise, students will never learn at the deepest levels.

Burden: High Complexity, Low Engagement

A burden is the antithesis of a game—very complex or difficult, and not engaging. This work requires carefully applying knowledge but occurs on a topic that doesn't interest the student. If the student isn't interested, he or she will not even attempt complex tasks such as research papers, multicomponent projects, complex mathematics problems, or high-level literature.

Mission: High Complexity, High Engagement

A mission is where high complexity and high engagement meet. A mission's engagement is personal. A real-life example is my mother, who spent seventeen years caring for my grandmother who was sick with dementia. In the end, my mother was there every day, showing her love for her mother. The emotions and difficulties of that condition made this one of the most complex things anyone will ever do, and my mother was highly engaged. At one point, my mother's friend said, "That must be such a burden." It may be for some people, but my mother never saw it as a burden; it was her mission.

In the classroom, a mission can take many forms. Teachers know they've achieved this level when they create these experiences, and students know when they are on one. Missions allow students to hit flow—a sort of optimal state of mind (Csikszentmihalyi, 1990, 2008). Flow is discussed in chapter 6 (page 71). During missions, students feel a high level of autonomy, competence, and relatedness; this is where a student is intensely engaged with a complex task.

Engagement Initiation

How can you juggle all these engagement elements? How can you create instruction and activities that land students on the mission point? The mindset-specific strategies in each chapter can help, but to start, break down your classroom approach into hook and context. A class example follows for analysis. This is launching learning for your students.

The following sections explain a hook and context, then take you through classroom examples from hypothetical educators teacher A and teacher B. Then, I'll provide a classroom examples analysis so you can see how the hook and context look in two different scenarios.

Hook

What is the opening scene in your favorite movie or book? Did the writer begin by painting you a dramatic picture to immerse you in the story? I think of the beginning of J.K. Rowling's (2009) *Harry Potter* series, one of my daughter's favorites. Three pivotal characters, with all of their special magical abilities, dramatically appear in the night and speak about the events that left Harry Potter an orphan. In this scene, Rowling gives the reader just enough information and clues to pique interest, raise concern, ask questions, and, most important, feel emotionally connected to the character who becomes the series' focus. That's a good hook.

As a teacher, you open the scene for learners when you launch learning. This is the opening of a story you want students to love. Dave Burgess (2012), author of *Teach Like a Pirate*, suggests blending one part content, one part method, and one part delivery. For each teacher A and teacher B example in this book, I will call attention to how each teacher introduces concepts, the methods they use to interest students, and their roles during delivery.

Context

Define a purpose before teaching a lesson. Without purpose, it is impossible to introduce a lesson and supply context. Students need to walk into a classroom with the ability to see tantalizing elements of that learning's purpose to hype their interest. Additionally, think about possible missteps or misconceptions students may have about the topics and prepare strategies to use or overcome those. Common misconceptions abound in science, for example—clouds leak rain or that you can refer to birds, fish, or insects as animals (Thompson & Logue, 2006). In English language arts, the subject that I taught, it was common for students to incorrectly perceive words. Knowing this, I often reviewed a text's vocabulary before we started reading. Without doing so, the context I set up could have confused and then dissuaded a student from learning. You can also turn their misconceptions into launching gold. Puzzling situations can create curiosity.

Fisher and Frey (2015) clearly state that

> effective teachers create memorable events throughout their lessons to capture student attention. However, it is important to note that gaining attention is intended not to provide entertainment for students but to scaffold learning so that the cognitive responsibility for learning shifts to the student. (p. 56)

Creativity throughout a lesson, while learning is consolidated, is important too. When teachers follow a bland teacher manual, students see "the teacher being lazy; students then have little motivation to complete academic work, much less become excited about it" (Schussler, 2009, p. 118). They reciprocate with their own lack of creativity and effort; they reciprocate with disengagement. Hook your students. Set the context and keep their interest up throughout a lesson.

The following classroom examples show two different teachers' approaches to *Romeo and Juliet* (Shakespeare, 1973).

Teacher A

All the students come into teacher A's classroom. The plays are neatly on each desk. Teacher A instructs students to silently read the opening lines in act 1. They comply but find the language slightly challenging. The teacher begins a minilesson on the Montagues and Capulets, Verona and its location, and the historical time in which the play was written. Students ask questions about what they read to clarify misunderstandings.

Teacher B

In teacher B's class, the teacher greets students at the door and deals one red or black card from a shuffled deck to each student. The students find the seats pushed against the walls. The front board says that students should form groups of between three and seven so their card numbers equal thirty. This activity makes students talk as a warm-up to the coming collaborative activity.

The bell rings, and students spend a little more time working out their groups. When those are settled, teacher B instructs them to take on the roles of Romeo and Juliet's parents and other Montague and Capulet family members. The red cards are the Capulets, and the black cards are the Montagues. Face cards are the parents and siblings, and number cards are aunts, uncles, and cousins. The families with red cards (the Capulets) get the task of developing reasons why Juliet is too good for Romeo, and the families with black cards (the Montagues) are to develop reasons why Romeo could find a much better wife than Juliet. After allowing the students time to explore the concepts, the teacher brings the room back to order and asks to hear some of the students' ideas.

Once the room is full of drama, teacher B decides which are the best (but possibly irrational) reasons. He asks students to write the reasons on the board by each group's face cards or the closest family members to Romeo and Juliet. Students push their desks back into their places, and the teacher invites conversation about the experiences students used as the bases for their arguments: were these things the students had heard about their boyfriend or girlfriend? Have they ever thrown shade at (shown contempt for) one of their brother's, sister's, or friend's special friends?

Classroom Examples Analysis

Which class do you think will engage more in the lesson? Which had an opportunity to engage each other and explore an emotion that will help them understand (and remember) the play? Which teacher allows students to discover what they might already know about the play or the characters' behaviors? Which teacher began with a game, and which began with a chore?

From a traditional standpoint, teacher A does nothing wrong. However, teacher B sets a totally different stage. His students may have gained the first insight about why Shakespeare remains important: he wrote about basic human emotions. Teacher A *told* her students how the characters feel. Teacher B encourages his students *to feel* what the characters feel. Teacher B launches the lesson; teacher A introduces it. Even though teacher B's students have not read a word of *Romeo and Juliet*, they have a kernel of the irrational anger the families have for each other, which, during the climax, is the reason for the tragedy. In this example, the hook was the fun game and energetic Romeo-blasting activity. Understanding the drama behind the play was the context the students received. Many students think *Romeo and Juliet* is just some old, boring story that doesn't connect to their current experience, but the opposite is true. Insults are hurled, fights ensue, and two star-crossed lovers fight their own families to fall in love. The context for the rest of the study is set by dispelling a myth that Shakespeare is boring and not applicable to them.

Both teachers rightfully assume that most students have a preconceived notion about Shakespeare, maybe even considering his writing (without having read it) boring. Teacher B helps dispel that assumption. Teachers should identify the type of social interactions and thought processes for students to engage with the content and each other. If your students think something is boring, trivial, or not related to their interests, you must show them when you launch the lesson that this is not the fact. As teachers, we determine how to invite the students into the learning. It is critical for a teacher to kindle the interests of students. As teachers we need to ask, "What is the hook that will grab their attention?"

Would teacher B's students' affect be impacted if he opened only *this* unit in that engaging way? No. Connection doesn't occur following a single instance.

Summary

This chapter introduced student engagement's structure and language. Engagement is something teachers know when they see, and students know when they feel, but can be hard to capture. During the next five chapters, I will apply these concepts to the student engagement mindset, helping you recognize and diagnose your students' greatest academic needs.

CHAPTER 2

THE AGITATOR MINDSET

Every teacher in the world has had students with the agitator mindset. These students' behavior disrupts class, foiling the teacher's opportunity to educate. The teacher engrains these students' names in his or her mind. I met my first student with an agitator mindset when I was a student teacher in a fifth-grade class. Brad was tall, energetic, intelligent, and compulsive. His teacher had moved him to every corner of the room to sit with a combination of students around him to inspire a behavior change. Brad interrupted everyone's learning. The morning I began student teaching, Brad was in his new assigned seat—by the floor next to the teacher's desk. It was only early September.

Brad did not do most of his work. The work he did was rushed and incomplete. Brad did not stay in his seat. Brad would joke about the classmates around him. He joked about the teacher and me. He was disengaged from the content, his classmates, and his teacher.

One of my first responsibilities was to take him to the gym so he could run around. The idea was that if we tired him out, he might get down to work. He didn't. I did not know how to engage with him. In fact, my first thought was to send him to the hall or the principal's office. The school suspended Brad often. Typically, I (the student teacher) would reprimand him. Then, my supervising teacher would reprimand him, call his parents and finally, send Brad to the office if the earlier attempts at discipline were unsuccessful. The school would suspend Brad if the teacher sent him to the office a second time during the day.

Brad frustrated me. I did not have the tools to engage and teach him. He took up enormous amounts of time, and, took time from other students. I did not understand the student engagement mindset continuum at that point. Brad had an agitator mindset, meaning he possessed leadership abilities but lacked self-control, was argumentative, and didn't complete his work.

I'll tell you more about the characteristics of the agitator mindset and how to reach those students with autonomy, competence, and relatedness.

Characteristics of the Agitator Mindset

Students with the agitator mindset are the least engaged. (See figure I.2 on page 8.) To be clear, these students do have self-control issues. In fact, their mission is to disrupt. I will explain why they feel that way later in this chapter.

Professor of counseling and special education Thomas W. Farmer and his colleagues (2011) refer to what I frame as the agitator mindset as *aggressive high-risk profile*. These students are in danger of becoming totally disengaged. In elementary school, these students may appear before a retention committee. Their parents attend significant intervention meetings, or the school tests the students for an individualized education program (IEP). At the secondary level, these students may be close to dropping out because of frequent truancy, failing a grade level, or transferring to a new school (National Research Council, 2011).

They often show behaviors like refusing to complete work. In fact, they are actively motivated against the classroom norms for beginning, doing, and completing work. James J. Appleton et al. (2008) describe this as *amotivation*, or anti-motivation. They have a keen understanding of what they are supposed to do and proceed to do the direct opposite. They are argumentative and outspoken. They may attempt to rally others in protest with them. (In this trait, you can see possible leadership qualities. They are excellent at reading their peers, the teacher, and the situation.) They attempt to form a classroom coup d'état, organizing to take over the power structure in the classroom. They feel like outsiders.

Because they view all work as chores or burdens, those with the agitator mindset substitute learning with other activities. They lack relatedness and therefore don't value the work, or these students feel incompetent and unable to do the work. The behavior may come from different origins. Missing skills, where they are hiding academic shortcomings, is one origin. Consider investigating a disengaged, disruptive student's file for clues and possible avenues to help. More often than not, however, students with the agitator mindset have the ability but lack initiative. Some are bored. They score high on cognitive assessments or standardized tests but feel stifled in class.

Agitator behavior may happen for two reasons: (1) a fixed mindset (believing that they can't change their intelligence) and (2) trauma.

Fixed Mindset

Students with an agitator mindset need something external to regulate their behavior. Depending on their agreed-on systems, these students may not receive rewards for good behavior. Traditional classroom-level positive behavior supports may not help, such as behavioral flip charts. Often when I interacted with one of these students as teacher or principal, any outward signs of negative feedback began a downward spiral of behavior. There is a chance such students will view negative behavior as a badge of honor.

Author Carol S. Dweck's research can provide behavioral guidance for those students. In *Mindset: The New Psychology of Success*, Dweck (2006) writes that how we think about our experiences, including successes and failures, impacts our motivation. She writes about two mindsets: (1) growth mindset and (2) fixed mindset.

Students with a growth mindset view failure as a chance to grow. It is a view that intelligence is not fixed but something that develops with time and effort. Students with a fixed mindset view intelligence as inalterable—they either have it or they don't. They see failure as stupidity. Challenges are dangerous because they can expose a seeming lack of intelligence. Working in a classroom is a risky endeavor because they might learn that they are incompetent. A student with a fixed mindset views work through the lens of external motivation, carrots and sticks (Dweck, 2006).

Using this mindset language with students has power. The advantages to a growth mindset are apparent to them. With this attention to metacognition, they begin viewing their work—and the world—differently. However, students with the agitator mindset cannot change their mindset until they view school work as meaningful to them. The section How to Reach Them: Autonomy, Competence, and Relatedness for Students With the Agitator Mindset (page 31) addresses how to help these students do that.

Trauma

Trauma can be the origin of some problematic behavior. NCES (2013) reports that 20 percent of students live in poverty and are eligible for free or reduced-price lunches. Poverty is a form of trauma (Collins, 2015) and can make it tough for a student to regulate his or her emotions or relate emotionally to others (Bell, Limberg, & Robinson, 2013). Keep this in mind when identifying those with the agitator mindset.

Also bear in mind the link between disproportionate suspensions, expulsions, and dropouts for students of color and the link between ethnicity and poverty (Shifrer, Muller, & Callahan, 2011; U.S. Government Accountability Office, 2018). Suspensions and expulsions do not acknowledge the rigorous instruction or social-emotional help a struggling student needs, nor do they acknowledge the bias that taints the interaction some teachers have with their students of color, students from low-income families, or both.

Educator and author Richard DuFour (2012) says, "All systems are perfectly aligned for their outcomes." Rich, Cox, and Bloch (2016), in *The New York Times*, confirm substantial gaps between white students and their black and Latino classmates, reporting that the "gaps are largest in places with large economic disparities." Its statistics show what the U.S. education system is aligned to do. How can a student feel connected when he or she sees academic outputs favoring one population? This is a topic other authors have addressed well, and I mention it here to highlight the engagement gap many students feel. If you are interested in learning more about the achievement gap, I suggest the book *Overcoming the Achievement Gap Trap* by Anthony Muhammad (2015).

Look carefully at the student's life experience, and use empathy to try to understand that perspective. When you learn that a student has experienced trauma, strongly consider using resources such as the following to research and then employ trauma-informed instruction: "9 Key Resources on Trauma-Informed Schools" by Lauren Brown West-Rosenthal (2017); *Poor Students, Rich Teaching* by Eric Jensen (2016); or *An Educator's Guide to Schoolwide Positive Behavioral Interventions and Supports* by Jason E. Harlacher and Billie Jo Rodriguez (2018). Trauma-informed instruction is a powerful tool to help struggling students.

When were you the agitator? Why were you the agitator? Was it because you felt like an outsider or that others in the group had advantages? Have you felt marginalized in a system with an established hierarchy? Finally, have you felt disconnected when you weren't given autonomy?

It is important to remember that helping students with the agitator mindset is not something that occurs effortlessly or with one heartfelt conversation. There is no consequence in the system that will change their behavior. It is a process to help them gain motivation. The research tells us that students with the agitator mindset need external regulation to gain motivation (Saeed & Zyngier, 2012). Sadly, for these students, that motivation will not come from home. Their parents are generally aloof or even side with the student even in extreme cases. For example, I had a combative student while teaching middle school. Because of the master schedule, we only spent the first ten minutes of each day together. Just a week into the school year, I emailed her parent kindly detailing the issue and requesting that she discuss with her daughter what they thought was ideal classroom behavior. I concluded by mentioning that it was going to be a great year. Despite my positively worded email, I received a two-thousand word response in which the parent defended her daughter's poor behavior (and another such email a day later). It was clear that I did not have parental support. I focused on building a relationship with the student; eventually the behavior stopped. For the agitator mindset, external motivation from parents or the school can happen and it scaffolds student engagement. *External motivation* is where a student's motivation is not internalized as either a carrot, stick, or positive feeling; someone is making them behave. As a teacher, you surely know all about this. Some students who have agitator mindsets need constant support to keep them learning. External motivation is artificial; the student is not in control of his or her own engagement. The fact is teachers simply can't provide that. Instead, we want students to become more organically engaged. In the next section, you will find the steps necessary to help an agitator become intrinsically motivated and fully engaged.

How to Reach Them: Autonomy, Competence, and Relatedness for Students With the Agitator Mindset

Students with the agitator mindset are in critical need of enhanced relatedness. For this to happen, as educators we must first examine ourselves, because "any effort to re-engage disengaged students must begin by addressing negative perceptions" (Adelman & Taylor, 2006, p. 64). We must challenge our own feelings, biases, and misperceptions before we can truly relate to and help students with whom we struggle. Educational equity writer Shane Safir (2016) suggests asking yourself, "'What are my biases toward this person? How can I disrupt my autopilot thoughts so that I can genuinely see and listen to him or her?' With awareness, you can replace biases with receptive listening and affirming thoughts."

In the classroom, the most important thing we must do to engage our struggling students is develop real relationships with them. They need to feel the sense of autonomy that empowers them. Autonomy is important for everyone, but those students with the agitator mindset have generally been stripped of control by teachers and administrators attempting to modify behavior—made to sit in certain areas of the room, denied recess, and given detention or other discipline that communicates that they are unable to make decisions. These messages put them at odds with teachers.

Many students with the agitator mindset have the competence to succeed if educators can break the barriers between them and the process. With their ability levels, they can lead positive change instead of leading coups.

Students need to think about and understand how they learn. Education philosopher Nel Noddings (2006) says that "no goal of education is more important—or more neglected—than self-understanding" (p. 10). Once we begin to understand how we learn, it opens up the power of autonomy, because we can see the path and know the pitfalls and potential successes. Teachers working with the agitator mindset must make sure those students understand what learning is and help them know how they like to learn.

The next sections will work through the concepts of autonomy, competence, and relatedness through launching and consolidating. My experience with Brad, who started this chapter, impacted my thinking and research so I could learn how to reach students like him.

Launching

When launching learning, identify your student's angst. Use what you identify, in a positive way, to reconnect him or her to the people and curriculum. Listening to students like Brad was my first step in changing negative behaviors. He felt everyone was against him: the school, the teacher, and me. I observed him on the playground. He wanted to connect positively with other students and was a good playmate. The students liked Brad on the playground, but they had grown tired of him in the classroom. When you make a special effort to connect with a student like that, students feel cared for and many return to their studies. In Brad's case, I wanted to find ways to connect him positively to the class and his classmates.

For example, I cast Brad in a play about George Washington Carver we were performing. I cast him as Carver to build our relationship. I told him it was the lead and that he could do a great job because he had the capacity to memorize all the lines. He looked through the play and then back at me skeptically—but he accepted the role. Brad probably learned more about agriculture, entomology, and environmentalism than anyone in the class. His natural leadership skills and charisma were on display. He quickly learned his lines and loved the scenes where Carver rose to save the farmers. His agitation diminished.

However, I caution that having students participate in one engaging activity isn't a cure-all. I did the following to continue supporting Brad.

- On a near daily basis with him, I referred back to the success he had while performing the play. I used that as a jumping-off point for polite conversation.

- I pointed out the other positive elements I saw when observing him in social situations.

- I started giving him some space to communicate, showing trust (that was reciprocal) and providing autonomy.

Although many different students may have feelings of angst, statistically, some students struggle more than others: students of color, students from poverty, and English learners. Shaun R. Harper and Sylvia Hurtado (2007) show that students of color who attend majority white schools feel alienated and lack cultural ownership, where the norms and artifacts in a school don't reflect that student's home culture. Poor students may be hyperactive because of eating inexpensive sugary foods (Jensen, 2013). Mindfulness activities like yoga and breathwork can counteract this by helping improve oxygen levels, metabolism, and cognition (Jensen, 2013; Mason, Rivers Murphy, & Jackson, 2019).

If a student comes to you feeling like an outsider, it behooves every stakeholder to acknowledge that and employ those issues as a platform for engagement. Research shows that examining social justice—human rights, essentially—issues in the classroom effectively helps engage disillusioned populations (Zyngier, 2011). Those kinds of topics include socioeconomics, ethnicity, and gender. These students may suffer from such injustice or simply feel as disaffected as social injustice sufferers feel. *Disaffection*, or alienation, can result in agitator (and retreater, explained in chapter 3 on page 37) behaviors and beliefs.

Students can use critical-thinking skills to view a capitalist society's distribution of wealth and opportunity, using a social justice lens. Teachers can weave in social justice issues in a multitude of ways, and there is not a specific method. The fact of exploring those topics might be the start that you need to reach your students with the agitator mindset. Secondary teachers can consider what text to select for students. Introduce text written from a disenfranchised person's perspective. Sherman Alexie's (2007) *The Absolutely True Diary of a Part-Time Indian* is a classic example; its narrator, who is in high school, experiences prejudice because of his ethnicity and socioeconomic class. Equating that to the real world is also helpful. Injustice still exists. Acknowledging that in the classroom is important.

Again, students with the agitator mindset come in all shapes and sizes, but they share the common element of disillusionment with school. If educators launch learning in a way that channels those feelings, they can re-engage these students.

The following classroom examples show two different teachers' approaches.

Teacher A

Teacher A is starting a lesson on *Number the Stars* by Lois Lowry (1989). Teacher A opens the lesson by giving out a world map and pictures taken during World War II. Students immediately go to the library to research the Axis and Allied powers, Denmark and its capital, and the Holocaust.

Teacher A advises students to work in groups to label the map indicating the Axis and Allied sites, share the best pictures, and prepare a short presentation on the Holocaust to share later in class.

Teacher B

Teacher B is also starting a lesson about the same Lowry (1989) book. In her class, teacher B has the lights turned off as students enter the room. When they are all seated, she projects a swastika on the board and says, "Tell me what you know about this symbol." Hands raise; other students shout out replies. The slides show photos of modern-day white supremacists brandishing the symbol around the world.

The teacher asks, "What are these people saying by wearing that symbol or holding it on a flag?

Finally, the teacher asks, "What symbols represent something positive in the world?"

Following a positive conversation, where students mention what they have learned from news or seen online, the class goes to the computer lab. There, teacher B instructs her students to search online for symbols that represent positivity or fight hate. Each student presents a symbol to the class. The teacher makes a special point to talk about the symbol and any special connections to the book students with the agitator mindset present, especially building to how Jewish people might have felt about swastikas and about the Star of David for many.

Classroom Examples Analysis

By grouping them, teacher A helps students collaboratively build context, as many of the book's concepts may seem challenging and unconnected from anything students were familiar with. Some enjoy working together, while others are less engaged and consider group work a chore. Teachers A's lesson helps students understand the context of the book in a historical way. It is not a bad lesson, but for the student struggling the most, there is no emotional relatedness. Teacher B's class gets to choose a symbol to discuss, which builds autonomy, and now it understands the book from an emotional level, which builds relatedness. Teacher B uses this story's persecution themes to connect with students displaying the agitator mindset.

Consolidating

Building relatedness with launching is the critical first step to engaging students with the agitator mindset. Next comes building autonomy into your classroom process. My student Brad was so used to being denied autonomy that once we had a breakthrough, allowing him back into the group to work collaboratively was a successful strategy. This freedom may seem counterintuitive at first. There is often a tendency to wait for a student's behavior to change before rewarding him or her with choices. Invert that thinking. Changing classroom instruction is a key to addressing problematic agitator behavior (Ainley, 2004; Riordan, 2006).

Metacognition—thinking through how one thinks, learns, and feels—is key to success for students with the agitator mindset. Research shows that it is especially helpful for middle school boys who exhibit behavior issues. For example, using "student perspectives as a basis for refining pedagogical strategies to reengage disaffected students" engages students with the agitator mindset (Deed, 2008b, p. 3). The following strategies can help the least engaged students develop metacognition.

- Think-alouds

- Graphic organizers

- Rubrics

This consolidation can happen when teachers have direct contact with students, during collaborative parts of the lesson (such as guided instruction), when students work together (such as in pairs), and during independent work.

Think-Alouds

During a think-aloud, the teacher assumes the learner role and struggles aloud through a concept during guided instruction. For example, when a teacher is working through a complex mathematics problem, she might show the problem on the board. As she works through it, she might say aloud things like, "I know I can't combine these two variables" or "What if I tried the distributive property here?" This think-aloud shows how one might think through a problem or text. The students and teacher interact during a think-aloud.

Think of it as a theater production in three acts. Act 1 is introduction and setup. Act 2 is about working through and verbalizing the important thinking. In act 3, resolution and learning occur. These are critical metacognitive moments.

Graphic Organizers

A graphic organizer is a flexible tool that helps students puzzle through concepts during collaborative work. They are like a thinking road map for problem solving and can help a group stay focused on a task at the same time.

Powerful learning occurs when students talk about their own thinking, and critique their peers' thinking (Liu & Carless, 2006). The best graphic organizers are those that make students question themselves, the concepts, and each other. Marcia Tate (2016), one of my favorite authors, who wrote *Worksheets Don't Grow Dendrites* among other titles, develops very strong graphic organizers. One of them asks students, in the form of a T-chart, why they use a particular strategy to solve a problem, ways they could improve, and the big takeaway from their work.

Rubrics

Rubrics are most helpful during independent work. It is a way to have the teacher's thinking open to students while they are working through a project on their own. Rubrics provide the boundaries for where a student is to finish. How a student gets there is open. He or she has the autonomy to choose what elements to work on first, second, or third. The student knows how he or she will be graded, so there are no surprises. Rubrics prompt metacognition when they ask if an element of the assignment is present. I have seen teachers post rubrics on posters hung for the duration of a unit (and write them on their classroom windows).

Summary

Like Brad, who started this chapter and was in my very first classroom, students with the agitator mindset are disengaged and aggressively work against learning. Educators must first know their students with the agitator mindset so they can identify why they are being antagonistic. Identifying that motivation is key to engaging them in the classroom. These students need a structured autonomy. Once you build relatedness into the launch and help them gain autonomy through self-understanding, students with the agitator mindset will move forward on the student engagement mindset continuum and experience greater academic success. Feelings of classroom competence align with the feelings they have about their abilities. And remember that a student with the agitator mindset may be the most competent student in class. Celebrate that competence.

These small successes can build within each realm of autonomy, competence, and relatedness and allow students to change. Teachers know this path is not linear. The little successes, like the one I shared at the beginning of the chapter, are always tempered with the occasional catastrophic failure. It is important to keep on the right path and not become disheartened. Just know that there has never been a student with the agitator mindset who progressed without the help of a caring adult.

CHAPTER 3

THE RETREATER MINDSET

Eighth grader Stacy sat quietly in my language arts class. I found out shortly after the school year began that she lived with her older brother, and her father, who had an addiction. Stacy did nothing in class—less than nothing. She completed no assignments. Asking where her work was, I learned, would lead to her acting out. Stacy and all of her teachers had developed an unspoken truce—allow her to sit quietly in class, and she wouldn't blow up. During a conference, her father seemed to care, but we never saw any follow-through. She didn't take part in extracurricular activities, and she didn't seem to engage with students, either. She seemed to be withdrawing from the world—but we had a breakthrough during a theater game.

Stacy, who had never wanted to say anything, was the first to volunteer for a character-development game called *teachers and students*. In the game, the students acting as teachers give one-sentence commands, and the students do exactly what they say—in a way. The students attempt to seek out the teachers' true wishes and use their words against them. They must comply, but they are supposed to flip the command. It's much like how the book character Amelia Bedelia behaves. When Amelia is told to draw (meaning pull closed) the drapes, for instance, she pulls out a pencil and paper to sketch the drapes (Parish, 1963).

Stacy volunteered to be the teacher. I was the student. We talked a lot about football and athletics in class, so Stacy was going to put me through a workout. When she wanted me to do push-ups, she said, "Hit the floor." Instead of doing push-ups, I balled up my fist and hit the floor with it. She smiled and tried to correct me: "No, lie down." I lay down on my back, putting my hands behind my head and yawning. Stacy and the rest of the class laughed at me. Using their laughter as a cue to keep going, I rolled onto my side, grabbed a coat from a seat nearby, and rolled into a ball under the makeshift blanket. Stacy tried to restart me with, "No, no, on your feet." I moved the blanket down from my shoulders and tucked it over my feet. By this time, Stacy and other students were rolling with laughter. I stopped, stood, and asked everyone to applaud Stacy, our teacher. Stacy smiled the rest of the hour. It wasn't smooth sailing from there, but she did begin attempting classwork. She began learning.

I'll tell you more about the characteristics of the retreater mindset and how to reach those students with autonomy, competence, and relatedness.

Characteristics of the Retreater Mindset

Students with the retreater mindset are within the zone of critical need on the student engagement mindset continuum. (See figure I.2 on page 8.) Students with this mindset habitually disengage from the work. They may have poor attendance and withdraw emotionally.

Students with the retreater mindset will not engage with anyone, not disrupting others, if you allow them. Sometimes they appear to work as hard as possible to avoid interacting with the assignments, the teacher, or their classmates. Farmer et al. (2011) describe these students as the *quiet* dropouts as opposed to students with the agitator mindset, who are aggressive.

These students are fairly easy to identify because of their body language (Black, 2004). They slouch at their desks, nap, watch the clock, sit quietly with folded arms, have in their earbuds, or are truant. Look carefully at the student's life experience, and use empathy to try to understand that perspective. When were you the retreater, and why?

There is little chance of them completing homework or studying for a test. These students rarely complete assignments outside of class. They view all complex work as a burden. They, along with students with the agitator mindset, take up the majority of a teacher's time in a traditionally structured classroom. Teachers can spend a significant amount of time checking on the assignment progress of these students. These students require a significant amount of your time to get them to work. Research describes this external motivation as *necessary controlled motivation* (van Beek, Taris, & Schaufeli, 2011).

It is important to understand the thinking behind the retreater mindset, and be aware that a single student may show retreater behavior in one class but agitator or probationer behavior in another. Most students who feel like retreating are experiencing the fight, flight, or freeze response (Barlow, 2004; Cannon, 1932). Students with the retreater mindset have entered a semi-permanent flight response to stress—assignments, teachers, or classmates. Klem and Connell (2004) say that "students threatened by a situation tend to react to a perceived failure by escaping the situation mentally or physically, and by avoiding or delaying the activity" (page 262).

From the outsider's view, all retreater behaviors will look similar, but it is important to know that retreat may happen for two reasons: (1) missing skills (real or perceived) or (2) psychological factors.

Missing Skills

Many times, this disengagement is a flight response that a lack of ability or a perceived lack of ability in a given class triggers. The expectation in school is that students should be performing at the level of their peers, and students with the retreater mindset see that is not the case for them. If there is no chance of success in the student's eyes, he or she will retreat and disengage from the work (Deed, 2008b). They will attempt work they think is easy, which is something you can use to help them have an easy win to build on.

Since they are missing (or think they're missing) specific skills, students with the retreater mindset may feel that academic success is just for a lucky group of students (Altenbaugh, 1998; Dweck, 2006). Dweck (2006) warns about the thought process in which people view intelligence as engrained and unable to change—"I am smart" or "I am dumb," for example. Sadly, this thinking can begin as early as the first few months of kindergarten.

The example comes to mind of when I was a kindergarten principal. We screened all students for basic readiness skills such as number and letter recognition, letter sound recognition, and first sound fluency. When we compared those scores with the students' ages, we found a correlation between those who were older and higher levels of success on the screener. Two months into school, some of the kindergarten students identified their peers as more academically capable than they were. Their perceived capability had nothing to do with intelligence or effort, but everything to do with age. The point is that students can frame their beliefs about themselves and other students at a young age. Students with the retreater mindset get stuck thinking they are not as capable as the other students around them. The strategies in this book, which include a focus on relatedness, will help teachers combat this thinking.

Psychological Factors

Academic gaps are not the only reason students retreat from school. Farmer et al. (2011) point out that students with the retreater mindset may disengage for psychological reasons. Social adjustment difficulties or depression are common.

Social Adjustment Difficulty

Relationships are hard even for adults with all of our years of experience, fully matured brains, and developed senses of self. Younger people don't even get to work with these advantages. It is easy to forget how hard growing up is!

During elementary school, difficulty adjusting socially can manifest with the feelings that the other students don't like them or won't be their friend (Lease, Kennedy, & Axelrod, 2002; Rodkin, Ryan, Jamison, & Wilson, 2013). Everyone has had this feeling one time or another, but research proves that many variables affect the perception of popularity, and that students in elementary school perceive each other as being popular or unpopular (Lease et al., 2002; Rodkin et al., 2013).

Puberty makes social adjustment issues more complex, creating entirely new sets of potential issues for young people (Brizio, Gabbatore, Tirassa, & Bosco, 2015). Districts and schools should adopt a good health curriculum (described at www.cdc .gov/healthyschools/sher/characteristics/index.htm) if they want to reduce the number of students with the retreater mindset based on social adjustment issues. Employing one reduces the rate of social adjustment issues (Centers for Disease Control and Prevention, n.d.).

Depression

Students with the retreater mindset may display signs of clinical depression. The *Diagnostic and Statistical Manual of Mental Disorders* (American Psychiatric Association, 2013) indicates that a major depressive disorder includes at least five of the following characteristics within two weeks, occurring for most or all of a day. Students report, or others observe in students, the following (American Psychiatric Association, 2013).

- Depressed mood, sadness, emptiness, or hopelessness, which can present as irritability

- Markedly diminished interest or pleasure in most or all activities

- Significant weight loss or weight gain or decrease or increase in appetite (In children in K–5, consider failure to make expected weight gain.)

- Insomnia, fatigue, or excessive sleepiness

- Restlessness or physical slowness

- Feeling worthless or excessively or inappropriately guilty

- Inability to think, decide, or concentrate

- Repeated thoughts of death (not just fear of dying), repeated suicidal thoughts without a specific plan, a specific plan for committing suicide, or a suicide attempt

If you think you see these symptoms in a student, contact your school counselor for guidance. He or she will have a protocol to follow that involves putting parents or the older student in touch with the right resources. Teachers cannot diagnose depression, nor do schools expect teachers to. That is part of why it is important not to jump to conclusions.

The classroom strategies I present in this chapter help students with the retreater mindset who have missing skills. I will not address students with the retreater mindset who have an issue with depression. That is outside the scope of this book. *If you suspect a student is dealing with a mental health issue, get professional help either on or off campus for that student.* The students and their families need help connecting to appropriate resources. Remain vigilant and advocate for students in these situations.

How to Reach Them: Autonomy, Competence, and Relatedness for Students With the Retreater Mindset

Students with the retreater mindset are in as much danger of completely disengaging from school as those with the agitator mindset. Educators should therefore immediately employ (or develop and employ) programs to help them; the program is a form of triage. Stacy, from the beginning of this chapter, was disengaging from school and the people around her. She needed experiences that helped her reconnect with school.

Like students with the agitator mindset, those with the retreater mindset need a large portion of relatedness. These students will continue to withdraw until a caring educator personally and positively interacts with them, learns their interests, and connects them to the content and fellow classmates. They need a strong sense of relatedness to the teacher, class, and content.

This is a critical element of teachers at all levels. Teacher relatedness is significantly related to engagement and achievement (Rolland, 2012). Research tells us that student-to-student relationships are critically important and that when students don't develop positive relationships with their classmates, it can negatively impact their engagement at school (Davidson, Gest, & Welsh, 2010). Furthermore, positive peer-to-peer relationships are significantly correlated with increased engagement (Furrer & Skinner, 2003).

How do you connect to your students? How do you connect students to other students? Finally, how do you help build a strong sense of relatedness to the curriculum?

Competence is nearly as important to these students as relatedness is. You can increase a retreating student's sense of competence by pointing out how much the student already knows and filling in skills, sometimes moment to moment. For example, you might say, "Rosa, you already know how to divide numbers, so long division is just the next step." Many of the strategies in this chapter's Consolidating section (page 45) focus on informing the students' skills or concepts where they may be hiding their lack of understanding.

One of the strongest strategies—formative assessment—helps those with the retreater mindset build competence during consolidating. Formative assessment includes getting feedback about comprehension during the lesson so the teacher can change instruction accordingly. When using formative assessment, the teacher takes constant feedback and provides additional and subtle support when students need it (Black & Wiliam, 2018). Formative assessment is crucial to teaching all students regardless of their mindset, but for retreaters, the ideal time to use it is during guided instruction and collaborative work. It is during those times that you get feedback, because there is a great deal of interaction and therefore opportunities to assess and modify instruction.

A teacher who employs strong launching and consolidating learning can get students with the retreater mindset to work, but only with focused attention, as mentioned earlier in this chapter. They have a low level of autonomy. These students will not work without extra support and focus from an external source. Beware of spending so much time with students with the agitator mindset that those with the retreater mindset (or other students) are neglected.

The next sections will work through the concepts of autonomy, competence, and relatedness through launching and consolidating.

Launching

A student with the retreater mindset feels safe on the fringes. Trying to incite this student with an intense or very assertive approach ends up in potentially alienating the student. It can help to connect to these students' interests and what they already know—but this population can be difficult to draw from its shell. You have to work to get to know these students.

A great way to get to know students with the retreater mindset is to do the following.

- Give questionnaires, asking "What is life all about?," "Do you communicate with words or with actions?," or "What is an example?"

- Play less-revealing icebreakers like those on Icebreakers That Rock (www.cultofpedagogy.com/classroom-icebreakers) throughout the year. (Visit **go.SolutionTree.com/instruction** to access live links to the websites mentioned in this book.)

- Use student learning inventories or informal observations reduces the retreater behavior (Schussler, 2009).

Most times, we reserve ice breakers and inventories for the beginning of the year, but "teachers must know students individually in order to translate their beliefs into actions" (Schussler, 2009, p. 117). In other words, a teacher cannot incorporate a student's interests—apply relatedness—into instruction until he or she knows the student. Students change so much during an academic year. A single getting-to-know-you effort can't accurately show all interests and skills. Redoing these activities allows a teacher to constantly regroup the students' interests to the upcoming learning. My wife gags at the thought of giving yet another questionnaire to students, but they welcome the activity. Teachers at her alternative high school had off-site days where students and teachers shared experiences in a conference format with the focus on issues that teens deal with.

Double down, invest as much as you can, on strategies to get to know students. In my classroom, I used brief theater games to build relatedness, and I frequently used new ones. My favorite was two truths and one lie, where students had to tell three things about themselves to that effect—two true things, one lie. The class voted on which is the lie. Kids love sharing about themselves, and you get to learn who they are and the connections between students in the classroom. We opened or closed classes with different games multiple times per week. You can search online for more theater or drama games.

When launching a lesson, it is critically important that you display enthusiasm for authentic content because it increases student engagement (Kunter et al., 2008). Everyone shows enthusiasm a different way, but we all know it when we see it. You should ask yourself, "How do my students demonstrate enthusiasm? What do they say when they are excited about something?" When launching learning, make sure the context you set is about finding where student understanding is and building on that to create competence. By doing so, students with the retreater mindset will invest in the lesson (Schussler, 2009).

The following classroom examples show two different teachers' approaches.

Teacher A

Teacher A welcomes students warmly as they enter and asks them to pull out the textbooks. They do so, and teacher A begins the minilesson with example problems from the textbook, referring back to the pages in the teacher's manual. Students read examples aloud. Teacher A instructs students to take out their workbooks and begin the lesson.

Teacher B

Teacher B gives a questionnaire at the beginning of the year to learn her students' hobbies. When looking back on these data, she finds that a particular group, who has been disengaging, lists learning about fast cars as their hobby. For this lesson, she gives out cards that have pictures of the fastest cars in the world.

She asks students to find others who have the same card. Once she has her students in groups, teacher B writes on the board: *We start the race in <u>ten minutes</u>. How fast can your car get from here to Michigan State University's Spartan Stadium in East Lansing?*

Students begin working on the question, researching their car's top speed and acceleration and the routes to East Lansing. The teacher moves about the room, listening, asking questions, and sharing great thinking she hears from different groups. She expresses amazement at any enthusiasm the students show about the cards.

After fifteen minutes, the groups complete their work. They present their thinking to the class, and the teacher kicks off discussion on which groups accurately did the work. With the work and teacher B's annotations on the board, she shows a short video from the production company of the world's fastest car. Students complete the problem and turn it in. She will use these data to find out where her students' understandings are of time, distance, and rate. To end the minilesson, the groups create posters with pictures of the cars and the worked mathematical examples. Teacher B displays these posters around the room as anchor charts for the unit.

Classroom Examples Analysis

Teacher A teaches from the book, and this is the expectation in some districts. Many of the students would engage with the work. I will talk about those students in chapters 5 (page 61) and 6 (page 71). Unfortunately, the students with the retreater mindset will not. There is nothing for them to grab onto, nothing to relate to emotionally. Additionally, this traditional lesson represents the direct instruction to the independent work structure of a traditional teaching system and not the gradual release of responsibility highlighted in chapter 1 (page 11).

Teacher B's connection to student interest and her open-ended question are more than just a classroom favorite activity that connects to interests. When a teacher purposefully uses instructional strategies, it increases engagement in students with the retreater mindset (Schussler, 2009). Students will also be able to mentally return to the lesson with the use of the high-interest anchor charts that they create.

In a study of over eighty thousand students, three-quarters of high school students say they were disengaged from learning because the material was not interesting (Yazzie-Mintz, 2007). Showing excitement can transmit that excitement to students. Student perceptions about a teacher's attitude are highly impactful to their engagement (Schussler, 2009). The interest built during the launching is how you invite students with the retreater mindset back into the learning when their interests and skills are a part of the lesson. This emotional connection strengthens a student with the retreater mindset's interest in learning and the teacher.

Consolidating

Students with the retreater mindset will routinely disengage from a lesson, and engagement is important. The disengagement creates monotony—chores and burdens that drive students with the retreater mindset further away each day. Make retreaters "feel like they not only belong in the classroom, but also that they are capable of doing challenging intellectual work" (Schussler, 2009, p. 117).

Consider especially what support they will need during a lesson and how you'll structure the lesson. Having structured protocols in which all students have a scripted job or responsibility is an effective strategy. If they know what their responsibilities are, they feel more in control—autonomous (Deed, 2008b). However, they may need additional social support within a group due to their withdrawn nature. Have support ready for class every day.

Again, formative assessment strategies are a strong component of knowing your students—all of them, regardless of their mindset. Specifically, for retreaters, it can help you determine how far you can push, challenging but not alienating them. Move about the room, talking to students, observing, and reading body language.

The following strategies can help you effectively engage your students with the retreater mindset.

Open-Ended Questions

An open-ended question or problem allows for discussion about how *students* choose to solve the problem, solidifying the relevance of the students' point of view. One of the best reasons to use open-ended questions to help launch students with the retreater mindset into learning is the possibility to harness and promote creativity (Ritchhart, 2002). They create autonomy and competence because there was more than one correct answer. In her book *Raising the Rigor*, Eileen Depka (2017) asks teachers to use questions like, "If you were the main character in this novel, how would you have treated your colleagues and why?" and "In your painting, what mood would you choose, and what color scheme would you use to portray the mood?" (p. 88). Depka (2017) explains that these types of questions "help support a climate of intrigue and increase the probability of capturing student interest," which can be part of your hook and also increase relatedness (p. 88).

Consensograms

Consensograms are one of my favorite strategies for formative assessment and to determine students' interests. They are quick, provide interesting data for a class to discuss, and are fun for the students because they are making choices. Simply post a question on a large sheet of paper or project an image of something like a famous piece of art, a visual mathematics problem like a tessellation, or even an animal. Have students write what they know about the question or image on a sticky note and place it on the image. Alternatively, you can have them write something about their feelings, opinions, or perceptions of the question or image.

When they finish, you will have visual data from the entire class on the consensogram. It should be reviewed with the class. You can create a consensogram from any type of content, in any class or course of study. Consensograms build relatedness among the group by allowing students to see connections between their classmates and themselves. Additionally, students with the retreater mindset can't opt out.

Journals

Short journal entries are a great way to check for understanding and engagement. Students don't need to spend a great deal of time working on these when the purpose is to gauge understanding. Do a one-minute essay or reflection on anything: the day's learning, a lesson, or a unit. The short time doesn't intimidate a student with the retreater mindset who may lack the feeling of competence. It is also private so it doesn't expose students to risk. Collect and read these. I used to put them into three piles after the students left: (1) got it, (2) getting it, and (3) needs help. I read and sorted these during passing times and put a star next to my needs help group. I then targeted my needs help group when planning upcoming learning or intervention.

Think-Pair-Share

When students are puzzling through a topic, play think-pair-share (Black & Wiliam, 2018). Each student takes one or two minutes to think about the question, topic, or concept. Then, he or she turns to his or her elbow partner to tell each other about his or her understandings. After learning from each other, the pairs then share with everyone else. While the sharing can get repetitive, I always felt it was important. When the students hear each other's thinking, it is a strong way to learn or reinforce learning. During the pair time, the teacher can visually check for engagement, listen for misconceptions, and help when needed. Those with the retreater mindset have an elbow partner, so it is difficult to avoid participation. Also, have students with the retreater mindset share at the end (after you have ensured they understand correctly). This can build their sense of competence.

Four Corners

This is a great visual way for a teacher to assess students quickly. I permanently posted digits from one to four high in the corners of my room. They were answers to a problem, feelings of students on a scale (with one equaling "I'm not into this at all" and four equaling "I'm really into this"), or understanding levels (one equaling "I don't get it," and four equaling "I can teach this"). I posed a question, and students moved to the corner of the room that corresponded with their answer. Students spoke with their feet, so to speak, and body language revealed engagement. Given their under-the-radar nature, students with the retreater mindset will not want to be left sitting at a table or desk. Additionally, there is safety in numbers so their feelings of competence or relatedness are not in jeopardy. You can allow students to change their corner if they change their minds.

A-B-C Summaries

This is a fun, creative way to check for understanding and enables students to share ideas. They go around the room sharing one word that relates to the unit. The trick is that, as a class, they have to come up with one word for each letter of the alphabet. Given the duration of this activity and how difficult some letters are, this is better done near the end of a learning cycle. To make this easier and to support students with the retreater mindset's competence, write the letters on the board and cross them out as students come up with related words for random letters. Go to the retreaters early or when you read in their body language that they have a response. Blend this formative assessment with a think-pair-share for additional support for students with the retreater mindset.

Hand Signals

Hand signals are easy to use at any point during a lesson to check understanding. This formative assessment strategy is something students with the retreater mindset can't opt out of, and it requires that they think about their own level of understanding, so they're employing metacognition.

In the *fist to five* strategy, the teacher asks a question or makes a statement. Students put up a number of fingers or make a fist to reflect their understanding (DuFour, DuFour, Eaker, Many, & Mattos, 2016): five fingers mean "I completely understand and can explain it" and a fist means "I do not understand at all." Fist to five ensures students with the retreater mindset are on target and allows them to see that other students may be struggling. Alternatively, you can tell students to keep their fingers close to their chest so other students can't easily see their responses. This can give them the confidence to be honest. For yes-or-no questions, use the thumbs-up, thumbs-down technique with thumbs-up meaning *yes* and thumbs-down meaning *no*.

Electronic Classroom Polls

These formative assessment strategies are about getting up-to-the-minute data on your students. With electronic polling like Kahoot! (https://kahoot.it), students use a device to reply to questions. These questions can be binary (such as *true-false* or *yes-no*) or multiple choice. Also, the electronic delivery systems are anonymous, keeping the student's confidence intact by not exposing a wrong answer. New classroom response systems debut every week! It's important to stay up on the new technology and harness their formative assessment power.

You can help the class with electronic data. When students see that their statistics drive the instruction, it creates a sense of autonomy.

Exit or Admit Tickets

There are so many variations of exit and admit ticket approaches. You can use an exit ticket at the end of the class period. Have students reply to a prompt or question about the content covered that day. They reply on a ticket and turn it in as they leave the room. You should use admit tickets at the beginning of a class or lesson. Give your students something that immediately engages them in the upcoming lesson. In the classroom examples in this chapter (page 43), teacher B uses a variation of the admit ticket (the card). I love exit tickets because students with the retreater mindset can't opt out of participating in the lesson if they want to leave at the end of class. The private nature of exit tickets allows for risk taking.

Fun variations keep it fresh. The 3-2-1 strategy has students write three facts, key words, or differences; two ideas, feelings, or similarities in the topic parts; and one question they have about the topic. You can premake exit tickets with fill-in-the-blank statements—for example, "I learned _____ during today's lesson. I still wonder _____." You can pinpoint specific knowledge that way. My all-time favorite exit ticket was asking students to use construction paper and markers to create bumper stickers with a short phrase from the day's learning. I posted the bumper stickers around the classroom, the school, and on the back of the principal's car.

Summary

For unengaged students like Stacy, school is a constant challenge where they do not find success. Students with the retreater mindset are in critical need. They may withdraw for different reasons, such as having missing skills or a psychological need. You should take both seriously. When launching learning, build on this student's interests and skills. Foster relatedness to the content, to classmates, and to you. When consolidating learning, create a perfect blend of complexity and support so students with the retreater mindset can make their work a mission.

CHAPTER 4

THE PROBATIONER MINDSET

Adam was like a flash of lightning on the football field. He was a scrambling junior varsity quarterback who used his feet more than his arm. He scored touchdown after touchdown for the team I coached. From those first days of August practice, Adam was a leader. It was not until school began in September that I discovered the type of student Adam was.

Football coaches do more than teach players a game. They are caring adults in a young person's life—a protective factor that improves a student's odds of resilience (Center on the Developing Child, n.d.). They help to build an affective connection between the player, team, and school—relatedness. As a coach, I had many conversations with my players, listening to their questions and difficulties, and helping where needed. This was important, because it was my job to make sure my players stayed academically eligible to play. This meant that a student had to begin the season with over a 2.0 grade point average (GPA) and stay above that mark during the season. Adam hovered around the 2.0 level.

As I learned from working with him, Adam was not as engaged with classroom learning as he was with football. Adam was a hardworking and capable thinker on the field. In class, he was doing just enough to get by. He completed all his assignments, but none at a superior level. Completeness was Adam's goal. He had learned that getting the work done was enough.

You can see the interrelationship in these elements. Adam was engaged in football, and part of that came from his relatedness to the sport, his teammates, and his coach. To keep being able to do what he loved, he had to engage in class. Adam did his work because football was important to him, not because he wanted to learn. Adam knew that if he didn't do the work, the school would take football away from him. He worked to avoid a consequence. He didn't have good connections with his teachers. Adam had a probationer mindset.

This chapter will review the characteristics to help you identify the probationer mindset behaviors. I'll tell you more about the characteristics of the probationer mindset and how to reach those students with autonomy, competence, and relatedness.

Characteristics of the Probationer Mindset

Students with the probationer mindset are right in the middle of the student engagement mindset continuum (figure I.2, page 8), neither fully engaged nor in the zone of critical need. In the classroom, you can easily identify these students when you think about their motivation. Students who have average or slightly higher grades but score below the average on the state assessments may have the probationer mindset. In many ways, students with the probationer mindset are like those with the aficionado mindset. (See chapter 5 on page 61 for the aficionado mindset.) Extrinsic elements drive both; students with the probationer mindset by the negative (avoiding punishment) and students with the aficionado mindset by the positive (receiving accolades).

They generally do not show behavioral problems in the classroom; they understand rules and follow them. They can be social with peers. If they get in trouble and receive a consequence, they usually correct that mistake but not because they are upset about missing an assignment or feel guilty for crossing someone. They see the mistake as something that hurts them. While working on assignments, students with the probationer mindset look for the quick fix to the problem. Researchers describe these students as *performance avoiders* or *challenge avoiders* (Bain, 2004; Meyer, Turner, & Spencer, 1997). They are very focused on their own internal needs. They don't have a strong desire to meet goals or accomplish great feats in the classroom. Their main goal is to keep out of trouble, so they can pursue what they want. Where getting sent to the office is the student with the agitator mindset's purpose or desire, the students with the probationer mindset will view this as the end of the world.

I identify with the student with the probationer mindset. I was on academic probation after my first semester at college. That experience helped me pick the term *probationer* and shape the description. To have a probationer mindset means you have something hanging over your head while you're doing your work. When were you the probationer? Do you see students with the motivation to avoid the consequences of your classroom or school? Is your classroom set up to have students develop a fear of consequences?

During high school, my motivation for engagement came from my parents. Adam's experience was not much different from mine. I was at school to play sports and be with my friends. My parents' clear consequences pushed me in high school. They helped me get into a good college. Unfortunately, I disengaged the first semester on my own. The daily stimulus of my parents' support was gone. This is an important aspect of extrinsic rewards and consequences: once they are removed, it becomes a sink-or-swim moment. When that moment came for me, I had the necessary skills to choose to swim. Even though I made it onto the dean's list numerous times, graduated college, and went on to complete a PhD, having been on academic probation helped me identify with students with the probationer mindset.

Probationer behavior may happen for two reasons: (1) a fixed mindset (believing that students can't change their intelligence) and (2) extrinsic motivation (to avoid punishment).

Fixed Mindset

Students with the probationer mindset have a textbook example of a fixed mindset, which views failure as an indictment of stupidity and worry about exposing perceived incompetence. In my middle school English class, I found that, when they answered a complex question (such as author's purpose), students with the probationer mindset scanned key words. On finding those terms, they would comment on that portion of the text whether it had anything to do with the original question. The answer did not necessarily answer the question.

They fear the consequences of failing at an assignment or class. These consequences can come from either home (a potential grounding by parents) or school. Educators want students to move beyond the probationer mindset. In secondary classes, however, a student with the probationer mindset may revert to the retreater mindset behavior after determining he or she has earned enough points in the quarter for the grade of minimal acceptance. All in all, the probationer mindset fears taking risks, but doing so allows us to step outside our comfort zone and grow. If a student is fearful of failing, he or she will not take learning risks.

Additionally, and as a note of caution, if a school focuses student attention on consequences, teachers may be moving students the wrong direction on the student engagement mindset continuum. Having consequences is necessary to finding the path to intrinsic motivation (goal internalization). Before a student can find intrinsic motivation, he or she must have external motivation such as grades, test scores, or accolades. Before the reward motivates them, they usually have to identify internally what is best for them and their immediate well-being—hence the focus on staying out of trouble.

Extrinsic Motivation

An unmotivated student who passively complies is at risk of falling into the retreater mindset. He or she has an external motivation. This means that some stimulus is helping them stay on track. They work with passive compliance (Saeed & Zyngier, 2012). They do the work and learn, but it doesn't mean they will maintain a positive attitude about the material (Adelman & Taylor, 2006).

Performance-contingent rewards may actually inhibit a student's growing intrinsic motivation (Deci, Koestner, & Ryan, 1999) and may stop a classroom from becoming a community (Kohn, 1994, 2016). In the case of students with the probationer mindset, who might have just moved up the student engagement mindset continuum from retreater, rewards can be helpful if you use them correctly.

Most important, they are using autonomous self-control. They are working on their own to avoid trouble. That means that, as opposed to students with the agitator and retreater mindsets, the teacher doesn't have to exert a constant control on the student with the probationer mindset; the student has begun internalizing his or her academic engagement. They manage themselves. They do so, however, not because they love learning, the content, or the teacher.

To help these students with the probationer mindset, you need to know the benefits and repercussions of two types of extrinsic rewards: (1) if-then and (2) now-that. *If-then rewards* are dangerous, and you should avoid their use in the classroom. They are extrinsic bounties that you'll use in the following way: *If* a student does a certain task, *then* the student will receive a reward. For example, "If you complete your assignment, then you will receive a piece of candy." Students with the probationer mindset readily attempt and finish minor tasks but have a harder time with complex work. What begins as a mission turns into a burden (Adelman & Taylor, 2006). If-then rewards increase productivity with chore-type tasks, but they don't assist students with complex missions (Pink, 2009). Also, since the teacher has incentivized the task, the student will expect to receive the reward the next time he or she does the same task (Pink, 2009). If you don't give that reward, then you'll lose the initial productivity you see in the student; the productivity can actually decrease.

Now-that rewards are different. These are extrinsic rewards that communicate that the student will receive a reward *now that* the student has completed a certain task. For example, "Now that you have completed the assignment, we can have an extra recess." You present if-then rewards *before* the task. You present now-that rewards after the task is complete. Now-that rewards are effective when given unexpectedly and are, therefore, not connected to student engagement (Deci & Ryan, 2008b; Pink, 2009). This does not hurt a student's higher-level-thinking ability or creativity. Now-that rewards create a positive affect between the teacher and the student.

Now-that extrinsic rewards help to increase a level of relatedness and are an effective way to help probationers focus on the carrot instead of the stick.

How to Reach Them: Autonomy, Competence, and Relatedness for Students With the Probationer Mindset

Developing a sense of competence in this student is the first objective. His or her academic sense of self is fragile. Anticipate student errors while launching a lesson. Model and communicate them to students with the probationer mindset. For example, when launching a unit on exponents and negative numbers, the teacher might say, "Now here is where I always messed up when I was learning that squared numbers will always be positive. You need to double check each time. But beware—cube numbers get really tricky when dealing with negative numbers." A kindergarten teacher, beginning a unit on shapes that includes rhombus, might say, "Class, if you have ever played with a deck of cards, you may have called this shape a *diamond*, but here is the secret—he has a hidden name: rhombus!"

Additionally, launching learning that strategically prepares students for the most difficult part of the lesson is critical for students with the probationer mindset. That way, when the going gets tough, they have scaffolded thinking to push them. It could be built into the activity or something the teacher explicitly says during the launching. Reflect back on the *Romeo and Juliet* launch (page 23). In addition to being fun and active, that experience helped students understand the purpose of nearly all the dialogue in act I, scene 1. At a time when students are likely to be confused by the archaic language, the launch empowers them with an extra understanding that will help them decipher the insults hurled by the Montagues and Capulets.

Building these students' autonomy, especially during the most difficult part of the work, is next most important. Peer-to-peer interactions are critical for staying on target during complex mission-type work. When a teacher makes it routine for students to work together, groups and the roles students play in those groups become norms. Students gain autonomy from their ability to effectively operate within those groups. Additionally, interaction between them and their peers helps push them to deep learning strategies. You will read more on this in the Consolidating section (page 55). Students with the probationer mindset will do the work and interact when they are in groups. Even though relatedness is not the most critical element for them, it is important for all students (Ryan & Deci, 2009). Lessons without collaboration put students with the probationer mindset at a disadvantage. The connections they build in their groups become a support for higher levels of work.

And finally, beware of focusing all energies on students with other mindsets. Students with the probationer mindset need help, too. They will probably stay engaged, but they need help developing a love of learning.

The next sections will work through the concepts of autonomy, competence, and relatedness through launching and consolidating.

Launching

Adam, the student from the beginning of the chapter, was a learner on the football field. Why wasn't he engaged in the classroom? Adam made it through, but imagine how much more learning he could have done if his teachers engaged him in a way specialized for probationer mindsets.

We have to help students with the probationer mindset accept that errors are a normal part of the learning process and abandon the myth of error-free learning (Fisher & Frey, 2015). There is no better way to do that than to model it in front of the classroom. Anticipate the errors they will make, and make sure that is a routine part of your launching learning. Take, for example, a launch on buoyancy. A common misconception about the concept of buoyancy is that whether something sinks or floats depends on its weight (Thompson & Logue, 2006).

The following classroom examples show two different teachers' approaches.

Teacher A

When students come into the class, teacher A asks them to copy Archimedes's principle from the board into their science journals. She hands out directions for the experiment, which includes floating tinfoil student-designed boats. The class talks about its boating experience. Teacher A asks, "What makes something float, or as scientists call it, what is *buoyancy*?"

The students share their understandings, including the basic misunderstanding that heavy objects sink.

"Let's test that theory," says teacher A, designating teams. They drop as many paper clips as necessary in the boats to sink them.

Teacher B

Students in teacher B's class enter to find a small pool full of water in the middle of the room. Images of different ships are cycling through a PowerPoint presentation: aircraft carriers, cruise ships, cargo tankers, and a submarine.

Teacher B asks, "What makes something float, or as scientists call it, what is *buoyancy*?"

The students share their understandings, including the basic misunderstanding that heavy objects sink.

"You may be right," teacher B begins, "but cruise ships are really heavy. The heaviest one to date is about 220,000 tons. That is about the same weight as a skyscraper, like the Empire State Building in New York. Do you think a skyscraper would sink if you picked it up and dropped it in the ocean? How does a cruise ship float if it is that heavy?" The students chatter about this comparison.

Teacher B continues, "Today, you're going to create cruise ships that actually float. Keep in mind there are a lot of passengers and crew on a cruise ship that really think you will ruin their vacation if it sinks." The class laughs. "Look, this is not easy," teacher B reassures the group.

To prove it to the students huddled around the pool, he constructs his first boat and it sinks. He continues making tinfoil boats and testing them. Each time he fails, he talks about saving each prototype and looking at what worked and what didn't. The students are eager to begin. Teacher B designates groups, and students begin working on the experiment.

Classroom Examples Analysis

There is nothing wrong with teacher A's launch from a traditional point of view. Many students will be highly engaged. However, students with the probationer mindset will do better with teacher B's launch. The entire opening is structured to allow failure and to play with the material each time you fail. The students who have probationer mindsets have been reassured that it will be difficult and that trial and error is critical. Teacher B's launch is a little different. Without doing the thinking work for students, he helps prepare students with the probationer mindset for the most difficult part of the lesson—successive failures. At the apex of the lesson, when the deepest thinking will happen, students need to shape their own boats and apply their understandings of Archimedes's principle. Teacher B already knows this part of the lesson will take creativity, synthesis, and problem solving. He preemptively supports the students with the probationer mindset, essentially frontloading the most challenging aspects of the lesson. When he talks aloud, he models what he thinks students will find difficult.

Consolidating

Before and as you consolidate learning, scaffold autonomy of those with the probationer mindset. As stated earlier, they need collaborative support from peers to help push their thinking and keep them on task. The most important element that you can have structured into your daily learning for students with the probationer mindset is collaborative learning during every lesson. Collaborative learning is a level of the gradual release of responsibility model for instruction (Fisher & Frey, 2008) where the students learn together. When students talk with each other through difficult issues, they have the opportunity to act both as teacher and learner. They support each other. Active collaborative learning is the key to helping your students with the probationer mindset overcome misunderstandings and provide them with the support they need to reach the deepest learning of the lesson.

Active collaborative learning increases the chances of a student approaching mission-like activity (Buckner et al., 2016). Additionally, when students are challenged or participate in complex, mission-style work, the byproduct is a feeling of competence (Meyer et al., 1997). This sort of learning also leads to higher achievement levels and autonomy.

The following are a few examples of active collaborative strategies you can use in your classroom that will assist your students with the probationer mindset.

Discussion Groups

You can find many great examples and variations of discussion groups with a quick Google search. Icebreakers qualify as group discussions and can be a great way to get the class talking. Graphic organizers and essential questions are two effective tools to help students stay on target during groups. You can give the students essential questions, but make sure they are open ended, like "Where are you most likely to use (*mathematics concept*) in life?" or "What purpose do books about (*ELA concept*) serve?" Share a funny or timely picture and ask "What would you say if this were your substitute teacher tomorrow?" or something else engaging, to get everyone's thoughts.

Matching, Sorting, or Ranking Activities

A properly constructed matching, sorting, or ranking activity around content can scaffold students with the probationer mindset through deeper-level thinking. When teachers focus on what the students already know and where they need to move their learning, I find this the most effective collaborative learning strategy. You can use manipulatives, which are common in elementary school, for matching, sorting, or ranking activities. They foster conversation when set up as jigsaw activities, where everyone has only one piece of the puzzle or solution. You and students can make these. It is as easy as cutting different concepts from a single piece of paper. When I taught students how to write an essay, I typed one or two simple essays about recent school events, including the activities and student names (which they loved), cut out each paragraph, and mixed up the strips of paper. (I used a paper cutter so the students could not put the essays together using best fit with the cut lines.) The students would naturally work through the essay content and setup as they talked through why each paragraph went into its specific spot.

Role Play

Role playing is like acting. Students assume the roles you give them. My students enjoyed playing out a character's next step on his or her story arc. It was a helpful strategy for understanding motivation, behavior, and storyline. Role playing works in other content areas. For example, science teachers can have students role-play predator and prey or the behavior of elements during a chemical reaction. History teachers can have students role play significant historical figures and events, even having the students go off the cuff to bring in modern events to these historical conversations.

A high school American history class might include students role playing the public's opinions about the United States entering World War II, for example. The teacher can lay out the historical context and ask multiple groups to begin defending their appointed position with a pros and cons discussion. Every five or ten minutes, the groups can share new information from the next progressing year (1939, 1940, 1941, and so on). At the conclusion, the teachers and students find out when the groups decided to go to war and then relate that to the actual events that led the United States to enter the war in 1941.

Students may tend to repeat a role multiple times, even when given the autonomy to choose a different role. To keep it fresh, I assigned different characters to different cards and students shuffled and dealt the cards each time. A variation is to indicate intensity levels on the cards, with low cards being passive and high cards being more aggressive. Each time you deal the cards, students receive an intensity level or a side of the argument based on the card they receive. I always loved dealing the extremes to students who usually didn't fit that personality—such as when the higher the card, the most disagreeable you had to be. This really made for fun fish-out-of-water moments and opened students up. This is helpful in later discussions when you can communicate in a common language about anything from a character's personality or feelings.

Experiments

Experiments are of course popular with science teachers, but experiments are not just for science class. My students loved having a so-called snowball fight, where they wrote their perceptions on a piece of paper, balled it up, and threw it across the room. Have students retrieve the papers, read them aloud, and tally these anonymous data for discussion. This is a great way to approach social science and create data to form a class consensus. Ask the class, "How many books have you read this summer?" or "On a scale of 1 to 5, with 5 being highest interest, which of the following topics do you want to focus on during the next unit?" My students loved the active nature of throwing and retrieving the paper.

Close Reading

Close reading supports students with the probationer mindset through the most difficult parts of a unit. It starts as individual but moves to being collaborative. You can use close reading in every content area and for every student regardless of mindset, but for those with the probationer mindset it works especially well. Close reading has three stages.

1. Students read and re-read an appropriately complex and brief text with text-dependent questions. Questions drive the re-reading, and scaffold students by going from explicit to inferential (Fisher & Frey, 2015).

2. Students annotate their thoughts in writing, which Fisher and Frey (2015) call *reading with a pencil*. Nearly every teacher I know annotates his or her professional books. When I read used, annotated textbooks in college, I could have a kind of discussion with the former owner. Consider allowing your students to mimic that process in class during one of your re-reads. Have students exchange documents and maybe even highlight exemplars from the room.

3. Collaborative conversations conclude the process because "close reading is ultimately about discussion and teaching through dialogue with students" (Fisher & Frey, 2015, p. 74). At the end of the lesson, you can pose prompts like "What is the author saying by beginning the text with this and ending with that?" or "What would be an interesting follow-up text?" Your questions could take many forms. The purpose is to ask open-ended questions that prompt higher thinking levels and develop students' argumentative, inferential, or opinionated thoughts about a text.

These students need to know they can (and will) be wrong and that trial and error is a very important part of the learning process. When a teacher can model that as part of his or her guided instruction, it creates a classroom culture where a probationer can grow. Collaborative work is also critical for the probationer mindset. It gives them the support they need to remain engaged in the learning.

Summary

Like Adam from the beginning of the chapter, students with the probationer mindset are in a precarious place—in danger of retreating. Sports kept Adam engaged, but what if Adam's grades had slipped and he couldn't play? Would Adam have disengaged from school? These students are on the cusp of true engagement. They do what is required but are at risk for falling back. The key is for them to begin internalizing their motivation. You can help them move forward on the continuum by shifting their perception of engagement from coercion (working to avoid a penalty) to reward (working to achieve something positive). Extrinsic rewards do help proba-tioners move forward into the next mindset on the continuum, the aficionado, but we can't let that be the end of their engagement journey. In the next chapter, we will meet the students who have shifted from the stick to the carrot—the students with the aficionado mindset.

CHAPTER 5

THE AFICIONADO MINDSET

I t would be accurate to describe eighth grader Aaliyah as obsessed with her grades. In school, she listened to her teachers, kept organized, and always turned in her work on time. Teachers and the principal regularly gave her the student-of-the-week award to recognize her excellence.

Every day, when she got off her bus, Aaliyah made the quick walk home with her little brother. Although her parents were not home but still at work, unprompted, she immediately sat down with a snack to complete her homework. Like clockwork every day, even on Fridays, homework was the routine. If she had questions, she would video chat with her father. Unlike many students in her class, homework included studying. Before her tests, she independently made flash cards or study guides. She sought out her parents after dinner to quiz her on those resources. After completing her work for the day, Aaliyah read for pleasure or attended volleyball practice.

To her parents, but never to the teachers, Aaliyah would complain that teachers never posted her grades fast enough. She checked the online gradebook on a daily basis, even from her phone at school. The turnaround for feedback was always too slow for Aaliyah. Her teachers knew Aaliyah was competent and learning, so they didn't worry about engaging her further.

Aaliyah's grades were stellar, and as the school year ended, her father suggested that she learn structured content online. Her father wanted her to do computer programming and algebra curricula to prepare for next year. He requested she work an hour a day during the week, with a half hour of programming and a half hour of algebra. Aaliyah protested, confusing her father. For him, this was about preparing for next year and learning a new, beneficial skill. The removal of the extrinsic reward of grades seemed to remove Aaliyah's focus on academics. She was not in school to grow a passion for learning.

Aaliyah had a typical aficionado mindset: obsessed with school and the grades she earned. Many people think of students with this mindset as the end-all be-all for teachers and schools, but there is critical work to do. They are not truly motivated. These students seek rewards and if those rewards change or disappear, they are at risk of slipping into the probationer mindset.

All educators who have aficionados in their classrooms must help these students grow a love of learning. This chapter will teach you how to transition such students to a growth mindset and provide methods for launching and consolidating learning so they can become academicians. I'll tell you more about the characteristics of the aficionado mindset and how to reach those students with autonomy, competence, and relatedness.

Characteristics of the Aficionado Mindset

Students with the aficionado mindset are very engaged learners. They follow all the rules and have a strong affective bond to school. Teachers seat students with this mindset next to students with the agitator mindset because teachers know that they will not become distracted. They are involved in clubs and athletics—especially those where they find success, since they join to be the best—and the communities that assist with college acceptance. According to Ryan and Deci (2009), they have a strong sense of identification and have integrated all the school's extrinsic motivations (Saeed & Zyngier, 2012). A school's grading systems and awards have a great impact on their engagement.

Students with the aficionado mindset do well on assessments. They may seek outside support for important tests like college entrance exams or state (or province) assessments. In terms of assessments, you could characterize those with the aficionado mindset as short-term learners, taking in all the information for the test and losing it as soon as they achieve the desired result (Bain, 2004).

Students with the aficionado mindset are not without problems. When their engagement is disrupted, these students can feel great anxiety and even distress. I suspect many educators end up raising children who have the aficionado mindset because we are extremely knowledgeable of the system and prepare our children for success in the system. Have you ever been a little late dropping off your child to school? Has he or she forgotten a paper at home? Did he or she have a noticeable reaction? These situations are a big deal to the students with the aficionado mindset. Disruptions don't rattle students with the probationer mindset. Students with the retreater mindset don't mind being late, and students with the agitator mindset may be late on purpose.

When were you the aficionado? As a student, did you earn academic accolades? As a K–12 student, were you driven by grades? What in your undergraduate or graduate work extrinsically motivated you?

Aficionado behavior is often related to (1) external motivation (seeking affirmation), (2) both fixed and growth mindsets, and (3) self-regulation.

External Motivation

These students engage in mission-type work and will struggle through just about anything to achieve a positive grade at the end. Ken Bain (2004), president of the Best Teachers Institute, refers to students with the aficionado mindset as *strategic learners*. Students with the aficionado mindset have an *ego orientation*, or "establishing one's superiority over others and the beliefs [*sic*] that success in school requires attempts to beat others and superior ability" (Duda & Nicholls, 1992, p. 290). Highly competitive, they want to know where their scores are in relation to others in class. These are the students who share their test scores and could probably tell you each classmate's grades.

Teachers may consider students with the aficionado mindset as dream students. There is danger of ignoring this mindset's needed growth. They are great students but system motivated instead of learning motivated.

Fixed and Growth Mindsets

Students with the aficionado mindset want to be the highest-performing student in class. In that, you can see Dweck's (2006) fixed mindset in these students where they only value the learning as "it serves to aggrandize their ability status, not for any inherent attraction of the material itself" (Covington, 2000, p. 24). With that said, students with the aficionado mindset will share qualities associated with the growth mindset, such as increased risk taking. This overlap, which you can see in figure I.2 (page 8), illustrates the aficionado mindset's transitional nature. Students with this mindset are in a place on the student engagement mindset continuum that allows them to transition into students with the academician mindset. (See chapter 6 on page 71 for more on that mindset.)

Self-Regulation

The high grades and active learning that the student with the aficionado mindset engage in reinforce positive self-regulation (Buckner et al., 2016). As students become increasingly engaged, they are academically successful; that success positively reinforces their heightened engagement. The cycle reinforces itself. This is why once a student enters into the aficionado mindset, he or she can become an educational force.

As classroom workers, students with the aficionado mindset attack mission-type tasks with fervor. Given the proper types of classroom structures, launching and consolidating learning allow them to gain the deep understanding even at the most complex levels. In fact, students with the aficionado mindset prefer difficult tasks, tolerate failure, restart activities when they run into difficulty, and are flexible with the strategies they use to solve problems (Clifford, 1988, 1991, as cited in Meyer et al., 1997; University of Georgia College of Education, n.d.). We need them to find the feelings of reward within the process.

How to Reach Them: Autonomy, Competence, and Relatedness for Students With the Aficionado Mindset

Autonomy helps students with the aficionado mindset develop the necessary intrinsic motivation for learning. Strategies that, like those later in this chapter, help them use their self-efficacy and make choices can provide that autonomy (Snyder, 2012). In fact, limiting learning choices can move the students with the aficionado mindset the wrong direction on the student engagement mindset continuum. When a teacher allows students the autonomy to make decisions about their educational goals and supports them with clarifying questions and activity design by consolidating learning, students can begin to shift their focus from merely grades to a genuine pursuit of knowledge and a love for learning.

Roger Hart (1992), director of the Center for Human Environments and the Children's Environments Research Group at the Graduate Center, City University of New York coined the *ladder of participation* to describe different levels of participation and how teachers facilitate (or don't facilitate) those. The following lists them in order, from most to least desirable.

8. Student-initiated, shared decisions with adults

7. Student-initiated and directed

6. Adult-initiated, shared decisions with students

5. Consulted and informed

4. Assigned but informed

3. Tokenism

2. Decoration

1. Manipulation

Students at rungs 4–8 are at varying degrees of participation. Students at rungs 1–3 show degrees of nonparticipation. When they are at the manipulation, decoration, and tokenism levels on the ladder, students are not empowered and make no decisions about their own learning. The next section on the ladder indicates participation. Those levels, from lowest autonomy to highest, are (1) assigned but informed; (2) consulted and informed; (3) adult-initiated, shared decisions with students; (4) student-initiated and directed; and (5) student-initiated, shared decisions with adults. The highest three levels of participation are the goal when helping develop autonomy in all students.

The assigned but informed level has teachers assigning a task (which occurs in nonparticipation) but ensuring that students clearly understand the meaning behind that task. This could be as simple as stating the learning's purpose or the standard a teacher is covering. The next level, consulted and informed, is where teachers actually use student input in the planning. Like the previous level of participation on the ladder, students have a clear understanding of the learning purpose. On this level, however, teachers solicit students for feedback prior to the lesson design. Teachers incorporate student input and become part of the learning experience. For example, you can, prior to a lesson, use a K-W-L chart to ask students what they know and want to learn about a topic.

Adult-initiated, shared decisions with students is where true participation begins. This is the level where students grow their autonomy. The teacher develops a project using student input and interests, such as in project-based learning. The activities, goals, and grades result from shared decision making between the teacher and students. The students actually help determine what path the learning will take and how they and the teacher will evaluate that learning.

The highest two levels of participation—student-initiated and directed, and student-initiated, shared decisions with adults—have classroom direction coming directly from students. In the classroom, student-initiated and directed engagement occurs when students independently decide on their learning and the teacher allows them to develop understandings on their own. Consider the open classroom model of the 1970s and 1980s. I was a student in an open classroom, so from that experience I can say that when you encourage student curiosity, it becomes a driving force for intrinsic motivated learning. This method occurs in many preK developmental or early learning classrooms, when students decide what they want to play with and receive the space to do as they please. Essentially all elementary schools do this at recess, and it is among students' favorite school activities—because they are autonomous.

The highest level of participation brings everyone together—students independently developing interest-based activities, and the teacher supporting their learning. As a fourth-grade teacher, I once saw my students on the playground protecting each other from a mantis. Animal environments were a large theme of the science standards. The students brought it into the classroom after lunch. We spent lesson time learning about the insect, its needs, and the best way to help it. For a portion of every day for a week, the students developed a plan for the mantis. In the end, we created a sanctuary along the trees behind the school.

Students with the aficionado mindset have a strong sense of relatedness to the educational environment; they understand how the content fits into their lives and because they usually have positive relationships with their teachers, they want to continue that (Roberson, 2013). They also feel competent as evidenced by their unit mastery, good classroom grades, and high test scores.

The next sections will work through the concepts of autonomy, competence, and relatedness through launching and consolidating.

Launching

When launching learning for students with the aficionado mindset, you should bring them into lesson and assessment rubric planning. It's the perfect way to start from what students already know and intertwine personal relatedness and motivations into the learning. Providing more and higher participation levels gives students with the aficionado mindset the opportunity to look beyond extrinsic rewards and foster intrinsic motivation. Move your instruction to the next rung on the ladder of participation.

Learning to set goals develops intrinsic engagement (Adelman & Taylor, 2006). Let students with the aficionado mindset choose *learning purposes*, a term Fisher and Frey (2015) prefer over other *learning targets*, *learning intention*, or *objective*. *Learning purpose* expresses that the learning is relevant to the student. Susan Black (2004), a former adjunct instructor in graduate educational research for the University of Vermont, University of Maine, and Elmira College, states that having students work in pairs, develop their own goals, and assess their progress gets students energized about the learning. Research psychologist Martin V. Covington (2000) states that self-driven goals are a positive way to progress student thinking from extrinsic to intrinsic.

Lastly, connecting goals with the real world—especially to the greater good—is an excellent way to help students with the aficionado mindset transcend their extrinsic drive for good grades. Project-based learning works well for this approach. Help them see rewards beyond those they receive in school. Show them the good they can do in the world.

The following classroom examples show two different teachers' approaches.

Teacher A

Teacher A does a lot of preparation work before a lesson in ceramics 1. He plans a rubric for each element of the art project the students will complete. As students come into the room, they can see the posted rubric and learning purposes in the room. They begin working on their projects.

Teacher B

Students in teacher B's class see the following question on the board as they enter the ceramics 1 classroom: How does my art make other people happy? Teacher B tells the students to have a quick conversation with the people next to them about what they think. The question challenges them. Most have never thought about the work they do as art. After a few minutes, some ideas start to come out. Teacher B writes them on the board. When they give parents and grandparents their work as gifts is the most common response.

Teacher B says, "Let's do something good with our art and this project. Let's make someone happy."

She explains that she has been in contact with a local retirement home, and that its manager would like students to create a ceramic art piece for the residents. The students and teacher talk about what they have already learned to make in the class, the décor of a retirement home, and even how they might quantify happiness. By the end of the conversation, the students and teacher decide that they will make centerpieces for the cafeteria tables at the retirement home. Teacher B asks students to state their learning purpose, and they decide it is to learn how ceramics can make people happy.

The students indicate preferring to work in groups given the size of each project. They determine the rubric for dimensions and other details. Finally, they decide to self-assess based on the rubric and retirees' responses from a student-created survey they ask them to complete. Teacher B records the elements and posts them in the classroom.

Classroom Examples Analysis

Teacher A's launch provides a clear picture of what to do. The launching will also fall under the *assigned but informed* degree of the ladder of participation. In all, it will be an effective way to begin learning but would not help students with the aficionado mindset focus on something outside extrinsic rewards.

Teacher B approaches the learning purposes differently. The collaborative project development and rubric land on the rung titled *adult-initiated, shared decisions with students*. The teacher decides on the project but allows shared decision making for many of the elements. Moreover, the focus on moving this project from a grade to accomplishing something that will improve the quality of life of local elderly people is the type of connection that can increase the level of intrinsic engagement for students and help students with the aficionado mindset grow. Students are also more likely to put in greater time and effort when the results of their work have tangible, intrinsic outcomes (Covington, 2000). When students consistently help develop projects that are personally interesting, they will come to know school as a place where they create, invent, and take pride in their activities "rather than continuously chasing grades, goodies, and people's praises" (Pajares, 2003, as cited in Matera, 2009, p. 22).

Consolidating

Like the launching portion of a lesson, effective consolidating for students with the aficionado mindset must include a strong focus on autonomy. Students like Aaliyah, who started this chapter, can have their strong, developed sense of self-regulation fully applied when teachers give them the autonomy to chart the path to their own learning. The following strategies will help students with this mindset.

Project-Based Learning

Project-based learning (PBL) works well to engage K–12 students with the aficionado mindset. Fisher and Frey (2015) explain PBL as "tasks typically extending across multiple days and . . . intended to engage students in a highly relevant assignment to acquire deep knowledge of a topic" (pp. 85–86). Often, the topics are real-world-related activities (Krajcik & Blumenfeld, 2006). In elementary schools, this may look like an interdisciplinary unit where the students have decided to improve something at the local library. In secondary schools, this may look like an internet video campaign to effect some community social change. It can look like anything that interests or is important to students. Basically, PBL asks students what they want to learn. This mission-type work includes complex tasks and deep learning.

PBL isn't a single project that the teachers dictate, either. Researcher John W. Thomas (2000) says it involves student-led, question-driven, and real-world-focused questions. Students are the ones, with the teacher's support, who create the questions that drive the learning. Some of the best questions I have seen generated by students in PBL classrooms have been, Why is fire important?, How can a book change a person's life?, and What do movies tell us about our culture? Students with the aficionado mindset are perfect for engaging with driving questions. They have a passion for finding answers. Thomas (2000) says such projects can include "design, decision-making, problem-finding, problem-solving, discovery, or model-building" (p. 3). For a lesson to truly be PBL, new learning must take place during the investigative work. Students with this mindset have self-efficacy that pushes them to own their learning.

Depending on the teacher's and the students' experience with PBL, projects and desired end results can be teacher-initiated, shared decisions with students or student-initiated, shared decisions with teacher, both of which carry a heavy degree of student participation and engagement. They're making an actual attempt to solve the central question. Teacher-initiated, shared decisions with students could be where a teacher, who has a good sense of the resources available to the class, helps elementary students by sparking their interest with a field trip to a historically accurate farm and then drives student interests to help develop questions about what they want to learn about agriculture, farming machinery, or the growing cycle.

A teacher of statistics may use his or her interest in sports to help students develop questions related to the school's football, basketball, or volleyball team's success and statistical outcomes from each game and over a season. The students would break down and input the data, but then generate their own questions to test based on those data. Student-initiated PBL is akin to current advanced placement capstone projects, where students develop their plan for learning completely based on their interests.

Many times, students present their final projects as a solution to the school board, city council, or a local business. Imagine a school board meeting where elementary students share their process of building a butterfly garden, and what they learned from beginning to end with pictures they took to document their progress. Or imagine a presentation by a high school science class at the local chamber of commerce, where they propose a new system for waste and recycling they developed and ask a local business to install this process. Those presentations are very important. They help connect the efforts of the aficionado mindset to an outside goal, greater than any grade or test score. Covington (2000) asserts that we can foster intrinsic engagement when students conclude a learning unit with a chance to (1) share the results of their work and (2) explain personally and deeply why what they learned is important to them. Those two elements are key for project-based learning. Master teachers who use PBL know the keys to supporting students are asking them the right questions at the right times, helping students see the big picture, and helping keep them on track by staying out of the weeds.

Service Learning

You can help students' motivation shift from extrinsic to intrinsic by changing the reward of a grade to the reward of helping someone. To help guide an aficionado mindset toward intrinsic motivation, consider using a form of service learning.

This is a real-world application of what students have learned in your class. When they participate in service learning, they use those new skills not to receive a grade, but to help someone. Many high schools require hours of community service or service learning projects, but this approach can positively impact student engagement long before high school. Teachers who use service learning report higher levels of student achievement (Brail, 2016). Also, students who experience service learning in a class report higher satisfaction with the class (Waldner, McGorry, & Widener, 2012). Relatedness improves with service learning as well (Skinner & Chapman, 1999).

Internet-based e-service learning lets students from anywhere help others without geographical boundaries. Websites like UN Volunteers (www.onlinevolunteering .org) and Generator School Network (https://gsn.nylc.org/home) offer a wide range of opportunities for older students to apply what they have learned in class. On the UN Volunteers website, for example, students can help map regions of Tanzania to help protect other children, edit videos from United Nations volunteers, and even help write a social media marketing campaign.

Elementary students don't have to be left out of the e-service learning. The need for on-demand peer-to-peer tutoring is growing. You can set up partnerships with a neighboring district or with one across the planet. Students can create GoFundMe (www .gofundme.com) campaigns to raise funds for a local organization.

Summary

Students with the aficionado mindset are highly engaged but only because external rewards highly motive them. Like Aaliyah, students with the aficionado mindset are advanced and doing well, and there is danger if teachers are complacent about not developing those students' intrinsic motivation. We need to help them see education's bigger picture. They need help realizing that grades are not learning's purpose and that a love for learning and effecting change is the key to success. It is the key to help them move to the next mindset on the student engagement mindset continuum: the academician mindset.

CHAPTER 6

THE ACADEMICIAN MINDSET

Valentina was a seventh grader with a passion for writing, and not just the process or the composition of a story. She asked the most interesting questions about how plot arc impacts the reader's interest in a story and how character development is intertwined in that process. She found many of the class assignments too easy.

Outside of school, Valentina was a voracious reader of young adult novels. She had a different book with her all the time. What the class read over weeks, she consumed in an evening. Valentina also wrote at home, working on her own young adult novel similar to what she was reading. She brought in chapters for me to read. Once, she even skipped bringing in the simple vocabulary homework and gave me another chapter. She did eventually turn in the vocabulary work, but it was clear where her focus was. Valentina was more interested in the mission of exploring writing than doing a simple homework chore.

Valentina's comments in class were so insightful they sometimes confused many of her thirteen-year-old classmates. She was thinking deeply about the concepts we were exploring. I feared I may have been an obstacle to her learning. I needed to do something different.

She enjoyed one regular class activity—drop everything and write. At the time, I was writing my first book. My young adult novel was a high-interest read for many of my disengaged students. I used a typical coming-of-age plot with all the things my seventh graders were into: video games, basketball, and spies. I would even work on my book in class. The class and I shared our writing at the activity's conclusion. The class saw and heard how I developed the story, and I talked them through my thinking to build their metacognition about the writing process.

When I was nearly finished writing my novel, I could not figure out how to connect two parts of the plot. I let the students have a real authoring experience, talking them through where to begin and where to end. I assigned writing the chapter. I promised that if one or more of the students put together something interesting, I would ask the student and his or her parent or guardian's permission to use those ideas in the book.

The students really liked the idea of having their work in a book—autonomy compelled them—so they went to work. Many students did well, and of course Valentina's stood out. When she read it to the class, her classmates nodded their heads. I asked Valentina's and her parents' permission to let her chapter inspire mine. The plan excited her. It wasn't the grade that motivated her. An idea of hers helping me and ending up as a chapter in a book was what motivated her. Shortly after, Valentina asked for my permission to use an idea from my book in the one she was working on. Of course, I agreed.

Valentina's engagement was not based on the grades she received. She was excited about collaborating with me. The typical relationship between teacher and student changed. I became a resource in her growth as a writer, and vice versa. Her love of writing and its process was the center of that relationship. Valentina had an academician mindset.

In this chapter, the concept of true intrinsic motivation is highlighted and I discuss what it can lead to—flow. I'll tell you more about the characteristics of the academician mindset and how to reach those students with autonomy, competence, and relatedness.

Characteristics of the Academician Mindset

Students with the academician mindset are most engaged. They attack intellectual challenges with vigor. You could say that students with the academician mindset truly have a growth mindset (Dweck, 2006). They view mistakes as opportunities, and daily activities are potential-filled experiences. A student with the growth mindset views work as an opportunity; intrinsic motivation is a byproduct. Where students with the aficionado mindset view mistakes as negative impacts on their grade or a loss to classroom leaders, students with the academician mindset can find pleasure in befuddlement. In the research, they are referred to as *deep learners* (Bain, 2004).

In my experience, they sometimes have trouble meeting deadlines, because they want to explore a topic's deeper levels (such as how Valentina forgot to turn in her vocabulary work). Like Valentina, other students with the academician mindset sometimes skip the simple homework to work on something else. It takes extra preparation to meet these students where they are. The school where I taught used a traditional grading system. There, students with the academician mindset did not have the highest overall grades in my class. They score very well on traditional, non-traditional, and aptitude assessments, but they may not have earned all the available points in class. They are far more focused on learning than on the system we use to evaluate learning.

They also succeed on state-level, high-stakes testing. If your school or district operates differential ability–level classes, they will test into gifted programs. They work hard at the learning, thinking through all elements, angles, and layers of a problem. They complete all types of work, participating in both boring and exciting learning activities (Saeed & Zyngier, 2012).

They work effectively with other students, but their relatedness may suffer. Students with the academician mindset might have a difficult time fitting in, but rarely, if ever, show behavior issues. Some may find it difficult to connect socially with peers or may feel they have more in common with adults.

It can be challenging to keep students with the academician mindset engaged in the traditional school model. In many ways, the traditional education system works against creating the academician mindset, pushing extrinsic motivation via rewards. Beware that it can be easy to over-rely on reinforcement, even if they are aware of the importance of intrinsic motivation (Adelman & Taylor, 2006). However, students with the academician mindset report not wanting extrinsic rewards (Schlechty, 2001).

In *The Element*, Sir Ken Robinson (2009) says that finding one's purpose changes everything about a person's perspective. His or her engagement with the subject and even with life changes dramatically for the better. Robinson (2009) calls this an *epiphany*. Having an epiphany and findings one's element are key to the academician mindset. Will students adopt an academician mindset in every class or subject? Maybe not. It happens at different times for different people.

Covington (2000) states very clearly why it is so important to develop students with the academician mindset: "For generations, observers have extolled the virtues of learning for its own sake, not only because of the benefits of personal growth or enhanced well-being, but also because intrinsically based learning is the handmaiden to better, more efficient learning" (p. 23). If you want the highest level of learning from your class or in your school, focus on developing intrinsic motivation—students' love of learning—and providing opportunities for flow.

Intrinsic Motivation

Unlike students with the aficionado mindset, those with the academician mindset have both intrinsic motivation and self-regulation. You can characterize them as having a *task orientation*, which is described as "improving one's skill or gaining insight" as well as believing they must work hard and attempt to understand concepts, as well as work with other students (Duda & Nicholls, 1992, p. 290). Higher task-orientation levels relate to intrinsic motivation and engagement (Duda & Nicholls, 1992; Ryan & Deci, 2000b). Task orientation occurs when a student is absorbed in the task and driven to do so by a deep level of intrinsic motivation.

Students with the academician mindset are content risk takers (Meyer et al., 1997). The focus on learning sets them free to explore the content and not fear failure. In "Fostering Intrinsic Motivation in Early Childhood Classrooms," Martha P. Carlton and Adam Winsler (1998) find that students with intrinsic motivation tend to do higher-quality work, and that students with the academician mindset can also display higher self-esteem, which illustrates their feelings of competence (as cited in Matera, 2009). They may "be motivated toward the idea of obtaining a certain learning outcome but may not be motivated to pursue certain learning processes" (Adelman & Taylor, 2006, p. 62). The structure may feel restrictive. Try recruiting them to codesign consolidating learning activities like project-based learning.

Given that learning is a social endeavor, in extreme cases, students with the academician mindset may hide their academic interests or deep thinking to try to fit in. They want peer approval, especially during middle and high school (Silk et al., 2012). Finally, students with the academician mindset report higher levels of self-concept when they participate in extracurricular activities and when they support their classmates through collaboration (Cross, O'Reilly, Kim, Mammadov, & Cross, 2015).

Flow

Intrinsic motivation's true gift is the concept of flow. Flow is an experience that all learners can have, and the research tells us that students as early as third grade can identify and describe the experience (Gwyn, 2004). Students with the academician mindset are most likely to experience it. Psychologist Mihaly Csikszentmihalyi (1990, 2008) coined *flow* and defines it as the "way people describe their state of mind when consciousness is harmoniously ordered, and they want to pursue whatever they are doing for its own sake" (1990, p. 6). They lose track of time. Their skills and challenges are balanced. Constant feedback is key.

Have you ever gotten so engrossed in a book that you just couldn't put it down? That engrossment is flow. I experienced flow in high school while reading the book *Roots: The Saga of an American Family* by Alex Haley (1977). I had to read almost two hundred pages for a deadline. I looked up after finishing the book to find it very late at night. I felt energized regardless. You can incorporate strategies that challenge students enough to facilitate flow.

How to Reach Them: Autonomy, Competence, and Relatedness for Students With the Academician Mindset

The most critical need for our students with the academician mindset is a high level of autonomy. Once you launch the lesson, make sure students with the academician mindset have activities that allow them to search for meaning in the learning. For example, an elementary teacher might have students draw a picture that connects the day's learning to a part of their home life. At the secondary level, students may complete a journal entry at the end of a lesson to reflect upon what they learned.

Competence is their strong suit. This element is therefore of least concern. They want to share their competence and have it seen as valuable. The different levels of the gradual release of responsibility model are not set in a defined order or frequency. The end of a lesson can consist of guided instruction during which students can extend their learning and look for real-world connections. An appealing variation for academicians may be to have one of them play the role of the principal and guide the conversation.

Students with the academician mindset need relatedness with peers *and* with the content. Give them much social interaction with their peers. Put students with the academician mindset in positions where they can support students with other mindsets. The collaborative learning that should be part of your class every day is the best place for this. When creating groups for those collaborations, I highly encourage teachers to strategically plan those groups with a blend of mindsets. Furthermore, a common strategy during a lesson's collaborative learning portion includes giving roles to students.

As an example, when teaching seventh-grade English language arts, we did literature circles. You can use them so many different, creative ways, but essentially students are split into small groups to read, review, and discuss a chapter. Each student has a different job during the lesson: character analyzer, vocabulary recorder, summarizer, discussion moderator, and reader. You always want students to have different experiences, but academicians can be very helpful in modeling the more difficult roles in the beginning of such a lesson.

The next sections will work through the concepts of autonomy, competence, and relatedness through launching and consolidating.

Launching

Valentina, the student from the beginning of this chapter, had many interests, including acting and playing the cello. Those diverse experiences and her deep learning allowed her to see things differently. When launching learning, find a way for students like her, with the academician mindset, to see the content from a unique angle. This is a challenge for a teacher to accomplish, but the launching of the lesson is the perfect time. According to author and researcher Ken Bain (2004), cognitive dissonance can be helpful to engage your students with the academician mindset.

Psychologist Leon Festinger (1957) developed the theory of cognitive dissonance. Essentially, it is when a person's thinking does not match his or her actions or experiences. Take, for example, the teacher B launching described in chapter 4 (page 54). In that case, a student with a probationer mindset would experience trial and error as an effective learning strategy. For an elementary academician, a teacher can dispel a common belief by teaching students that just because something is heavier doesn't mean it will sink more quickly in water. The teacher could really hammer that point home if, after asking the academician to engineer a boat with foil, he or she exchanged the building material for a much heavier substance like clay. To build to that point, the teacher could guide a conversation and have the student predict the changes in the clay-built boat. These events challenge and puzzle participants; they prompt curiosity.

Festinger (1957) tells us that we do *one* of three things when we receive information contrary to our current thinking.

1. We change the belief.

2. We change the action, if it is in our control, or the behavior.

3. We change our perception of the action to justify our conflicting belief or action.

These experiences don't have to be long, drawn-out events. Showing film or video is one quick way to show students information that runs contrary to their current beliefs. That way, students can see things with their own eyes. These changes can be helpful to a student learning at deeper levels because they draw his or her interest and increase relatedness to the content.

Discrepant events are a good cognitive dissonance strategy. One of my favorites includes asking students to identify the Earth's rotation and then showing them a time-lapse sunset on the summer solstice in Alaska (where the sun never totally goes down). In an algebra class, the teacher can draw a graph on the board, ask students to predict which of the two equations the graph represents, and have them solve the equations so students can see that both are represented. Try seemingly impossible science experiments with counterintuitive outcomes, such as showing that a can of regular soda will sink to the bottom of a fish tank but a diet soda will not. Other times, try a re-enactment or simulation. Discrepant events in science or social studies class are common, but any content area or grade can employ them. Discrepant events also create a strong emotional connection to the learning, prompting students to remember these experiences (Fisher & Frey, 2015).

The following classroom examples show two different teachers' approaches.

Teacher A

Teacher A distributes a map of the U.S. westward expansion to arriving students. When everyone is seated, he begins discussing the 1830 Indian Removal Act. On the map, students can see both when the zones were purchased and the native tribes that inhabited those areas who were forced to move. Teacher A shows a short video that briefly summarizes the Trail of Tears.

Teacher B

Students walk into teacher B's room and begin working on a short worksheet about native tribe leaders, but the custodian—a secret collaborator in this simulation experience—comes into the room and says he needs the room for other purposes and that they must pack up and go to the gym. Confused and put out, but compliant, the students pack their belongings and go.

Arriving at the gym, students restart their work in less optimal conditions. The custodian interrupts them again with, "This room is too valuable; we are going to move you again." The teacher lets the students' murmurs turn into, "Where are we going? Will they make us leave there too?" Angry and tired, they dispute the custodian. Seeing their arguments are futile, they move to the library.

Later, the custodian reappears again to move teacher B's class. At that point, some students become upset and try to resist. They begin debating each other. Just as things become heated, teacher B stops everyone. He tells all the students everything is okay, thanks the custodian, and tells the students that it isn't the custodian's fault. He immediately ties their current emotions with the people who experienced the Trail of Tears (and clarifies that having to walk around the school is not equivalent to what the Native Americans experienced). The class then watches a short video about the Trail of Tears.

Classroom Examples Analysis

Teacher A begins with a traditional lesson opening. The information is clear, and the students have been invited to learn. In a much more dramatic opening, teacher B uses a discrepant event. Teacher B's launch really pushes students out of their comfort levels. The learning transcends a traditional classroom by including high emotion. With that emotion, students may gain a level of empathy and relatedness. That is a different perspective. Launching for teacher A and teacher B ended the same way, but teacher B prepares his students to think differently about the learning that follows.

They have experienced the lesson in a memorable way. This surprise has the potential to connect with the academician because of the discrepant event.

Consolidating

In *Unstoppable Learning*, Fisher and Frey (2015) cite thought-provoking questions as an excellent launching strategy. Using a thought-provoking question to drive instruction is very engaging for your students. Students like Valentina always responded well to deep questions posed to the class, including "How did this character's actions impact the most critical moments in the plot arc?" and "What was the author's message or purpose to the reader with the main character's monologue before he passes away?" This is particularly relevant for students with the academician mindset (Bain, 2004). Taking those questions beyond how we launch a unit of study is also an exciting idea and helpful throughout the consolidating portion.

The following strategies will support students with the academician mindset, and they both begin with questions that drive learning, collaboration, and creativity.

Socratic Seminars

One way to blend collaborative conversation with thought-provoking questions is through Socratic seminars. During Socratic seminars, peers teach each other through open-ended questions, autonomy, deep thinking, and multilevel structured collaboration. The multilevel collaboration is structured in the Socratic circle, where students are taught norms of listening and notetaking to respond and assist later, while other students are asking questions and answering one another. Socratic seminars are a great follow-up after students complete a close read (Fisher, Frey, & Hattie, 2016). It could be tough to do with elementary students, but you can succeed (Fisher et al., 2016). It can be as simple as asking "Who are the main characters in the book we read today?" or "What was interesting about our science experiment?" The process with younger students takes a great deal of modeling and time, but the fruitful discussion where students must formulate and articulate their thoughts is worth it.

There are different ways to do this in a classroom, but they all have key elements. Half the class sits in a circle in the middle of the room, fishbowl style. The other half is in the support role, with each student connected to a partner and generally sitting behind him or her. A checklist for participation is on students' desks, allowing participants to think about their own engagement. Supporting students mark the speaker's activity. Sometimes, one remark can generate multiple hits on the checklist. Figure 6.1 is a sample Socratic seminar checklist for elementary grades.

Student name: _____									
Put a check in the right box each time your partner does one of these.									
Joins in									
Asks a question									
Says something about what we learned									
Adds on to someone else's comment									
Comments:									
Ideas for next time:									

Figure 6.1: Sample Socratic seminar checklist for elementary grades.

*Visit **go.SolutionTree.com/instruction** for a free reproducible version of this figure.*

Figure 6.2 is a sample Socratic seminar checklist for secondary grades.

Student name: _____									
Put a check in the appropriate box each time you witness your partner doing one of the following actions.									
Participates in the conversation									
Asks a question of a fellow classmate									
Cites the text or previous learning in a comment									
Uses a classmate's point in his or her own comment									
Comments:									
Things to connect next time:									

Figure 6.2: Sample Socratic seminar checklist for secondary grades.

*Visit **go.SolutionTree.com/instruction** for a free reproducible version of this figure.*

This is just one example of what the checklist might look like; there is no *one* way to do it. Consider having students with the academician mindset personalize this checklist when embarking on this type of activity. They could decide to add a row for key concepts or learning from the lesson or for nonverbal expression or attentiveness.

A generally open-ended topic or question starts the process in class. (Middle school and high school examples include "Who is the most pivotal character of Herman Melville's 1851 *Moby-Dick; or, The Whale*?" and "What was the most important element of the French Impressionist movement?") The students in the middle of the circle begin conversing; support students mark the checklist and record ideas to give to the speaker later. Consider including an intermission so the speaker and support student can plan their next points of discussion. At the end, it is important for all students to use the notes they write to reflect on the experience. When you are done, students can reflect further during classroom discussion or by writing a journal entry. It is also important that students are allowed to experience both the roles inside the circle and outside.

Supplying the questions ahead of time lets students prepare their thoughts. Consider supplying two questions and not telling students which they will discuss, or providing the question in advance but not telling students who will speak and who will support.

Students who are unfamiliar with Socratic seminars need support. It can help if the teacher is part of the conversation, but the goal is to scaffold them toward independence. Move from "We do it" to "You do it" in Fisher and Frey's (2008) gradual release of responsibility (see table 1.1 on page 17). Mary Davenport (2016), teacher at Graded—The American School of São Paulo, talks about how she helps her students gain independence:

> I practice gradual release of Socratic seminar throughout the year. Early on, I insert myself into the conversation frequently. These interruptions can be feedback about strong performances or ways to improve, lessons about conversation strategies, highlighting impressive questions or insights, muting dominant voices, soliciting reserved voices, and/or pausing the dialogue so that students can self-assess and adjust moving forward. As the year goes on, these interruptions occur less frequently as students internalize expectations and step up as facilitators.

Finally, consider giving students with the academician mindset a few tricks for positive group conversation. For example, I am a big fan of the show *Whose Line Is It Anyway?* I was amazed at the comedians' ability to think so fast. Author Malcolm Gladwell (2005) reveals a trick about improvisational comedy that can impact everyday collaboration. It's called *yes, and*. The comedians never shut down an opportunity or suggestion. They always build on their partners. This positive attitude pervades the actors' interaction and affect. If you want your students to get better at their Socratic seminars, consider warming them up with some *yes, and* improvisation. It will also positively impact their feelings of relatedness toward each other.

Genius Hour

You can tap into students' natural curiosity and passions—in any type of class and at any grade level—with a genius hour (Smith, 2017; West & Roberts, 2016). Sometimes referred to as *innovation immersion events* (Ditkoff, 2011) or *FedEx days* (because you have to deliver an idea), start by simply asking students what interests them. From there, give them time to complete their passion projects. The high level of relatedness to the topic and to other people is a key component (Heick, 2018). This approach is another good example of *student-initiated, shared decisions with adults* on the ladder of participation. It also taps into a student's sense of autonomy, because it is self-directed. The collaborative relationship that a teacher has with his or her students during genius hour is similar to dissertation chair and PhD student—it bonds people together. Employing genius hour could help students to see the inter-relatedness of core content areas and see education's bigger picture.

These passion projects are self-directed, which taps into a student's sense of auton-omy, but as the teacher, you can do a few helpful things. Help your students brain-storm topics, allowing students to play ideas off each other. Consider leading a class discussion about your own passions and then asking students what they are passion-ate about. When students have settled on a topic, help them decide on a presentation modality and give them a research minilesson (West & Roberts, 2016). It is also best if you co-create a completion timeline that has small steps (Smith, 2017). Determine what content-area standards you can integrate into student work (West & Roberts, 2016) and commit a part of each day or each week for work.

Finally, ask students to reflect on their learning. Have students ask themselves the following questions about their projects.

- On a scale of 1 to 4, 4 being exceptional, how would you rate your effort on your genius hour project? What is your rationale for that score?

- What surprised you when you researched? How did it change your final product?

- If someone else were going to do a genius hour project on your topic, what advice would you give?

Once they have shared their reflections, celebrate your students' hard work. Keep pictures and artifacts to inspire the next round of genius hours.

The scale and scope of final projects vary greatly from kindergarten to high school. Two teachers from my district's elementary school did a twist on genius hour by framing investigations around careers. With their students, they visited multi-ple job sites, including an airport and a software company. The students created semester-long passion projects based on what they learned. The students were filled with pride when they presented their work to parents and community members.

Some innovations are directly related to genius hours. Notably, during theirs, Google engineers developed Gmail and Google News (West & Roberts, 2016). What innovations could your class develop if their passions guided them?

Summary

Students like Valentina with the academician mindset are intrinsically motivated to engage with learning. They are driven and passionate. Because they are such good students, you may be tempted to leave them alone to spend time with students who need more attention. However, it's important that you pay attention to these students' needs. Give students with the academician mindset the autonomy and time to push themselves. Give them opportunities to engage with peers. I think about students like Valentina and how, as educators, we must make sure to create classroom environments that intrigue, excite, and push students like her to exceptional ends.

CHAPTER 7

ENGAGEMENT CULTURE SCHOOLWIDE

Earlier chapters focus on grades preK–12 teachers. This chapter supports teachers and administrators, since principals and district leaders have a broader reach and can do much to establish schoolwide culture. Systematic changes precede culture changes. You can lead the steps to systematic change.

Here, I will explain why staff may resist change, so you can get buy-in. Then, I will walk you through the steps you'll need to take to create a culture of engagement in a school at large.

Resistance to Change

Why would anyone ever fight against developing high levels of student engagement? The short answer is that our school culture is deeply engrained and difficult to change (Muhammad, 2018). There might be pushback when your team decides on what strategies to implement to increase engagement. It is important to know why some educators push back and to help them understand their feelings of resistance and why they should join together as a team to implement new strategies in the classroom.

Some people resist new strategies. Changing how one teaches can conflict with the prototypes we have structured in our minds about the roles teachers play. This stems from our socialization. Work and organizational studies professor emeritus Edgar Schein (2004), organizational theory researcher, states that people reflect what *has* worked, not what might work for today's goals. Our educational system used to be about creating a two-tier system of educational winners and losers. Now, the primary agenda has changed, and public education is supposed to educate all students to achieve success.

All cultures will socialize the new individual entering the organization (Tierney, 2006). For example, a "socialization process in the organization causes the culture to reinforce itself and thus become relatively stable over time, and so builds inertia" (Sastry, 1997, as cited in Molineux, 2013, p. 1593). This effect magnifies for teachers. Nearly all people who become teachers bring fourteen years of preK–12 experience; four years of undergraduate school; and sometimes two or more years of graduate school—during which they observed school culture and developed strong prototypes of behavioral norms, values, policy, and procedures (Muhammad, 2018).

Unlike any other profession, educators have an extremely difficult time thinking outside the box. We were socialized in our field from the time we were children and struggle to implement strategies that conflict with our socialization. This phenomenon is called the *apprenticeship of observation* (Lortie, 1975). Dan Lortie (1975) concludes from his interview of a few dozen teachers that the public school system has a distinct culture and that it's the hardest culture to change because everyone is entrenched in this way of thinking and doing. This is the apprenticeship of observation.

Additionally, because most educators identify with the aficionado mindset, they might have a difficult time relating to the experience of other student engagement mindsets. Lortie's (1975) seminal research predicts that educators who succeed in the system subconsciously implement practices to protect the system, including rules and codes for students that ensure compliance. Watch for that in yourself.

You should anticipate conflict when adopting new practices within launching and consolidating learning. Ask staff to examine why they resist the change and to work to fight that bias. If they can do that and then pivot to focus on learning for all students, change can happen.

The Six Steps to the School-Improvement Process

Black (2004) encourages school officials to follow six steps to improve student engagement. I blended those condensed elements with the topics of this book. These are an excellent way to address the engagement gap in your school.

1. Focus on developing a school culture that centers on investing in student learning at higher levels.

2. Work with parents on the topic of student engagement so they can understand their own role in framing their child's mindset.

3. Use student motivation as part of the school-improvement and district-improvement process.

4. Have staff model and celebrate the gift of being lifelong learners.

5. Allow teachers and students a high degree of autonomy when they search for effective strategies, and share them.

6. Train, encourage, and monitor the use of effective instructional strategies like launching and consolidating learning.

The following blends these steps with this book's focus.

Develop a Culture Invested in Student Learning

Focus on developing a school culture that centers on investing in student learning at higher levels. Specifically, you can do so with two steps.

1. The principal or collaborative school-improvement team assembles a team that, ideally, includes teachers, parents, and students. The team members read this book and make sure they can accurately use engagement vocabulary and understand the mindsets' traits.

2. The team asks itself two questions:

    a. "How many students do you think are disengaged?"

    b. "How would it feel to be a part of a team that helps increase student engagement, not just in one class, but throughout a school?"

The following sections guide you through these conversations.

How Many Students Do You Think Are Disengaged?

Educators know there are disengaged students. Appleton et al. (2008) report 28 percent of U.S. students are at risk of dropping out; they're in the zone of critical need. Without intervention, these students—who comprise the agitator and retreater mindsets—will drop out. Not by chance, the 2008 graduation rates in both Canada and the United States were around 72 percent (Koebler, 2011; Statistics Canada, 2015).

Regardless of whether teachers know some students are disengaged, it is critical that teachers have the chance to verbalize this. Verbalization is both a form of reflective practice for problem solving (Clarke, 2011) and helpful when initially solving complex problems that need strategic methods (Ahlum-Heath & Di Vesta, 1986). After staff say aloud that they have disengaged students who need help, it is time to dig down into the school's engagement culture. For each class, each teacher should complete the student engagement mindset assessment in figure 7.1 (page 86). Teachers will record what mindset they think each student displays. It may be helpful to have class lists available, but *it is critical that you do not write students' names on this sheet*. Instead of writing names, give each student an identifying number, and record those instead. Secondary school teachers should do this in grade-level teams or interdisciplinary teams. Include teachers of music, art, foreign language, and physical education.

Continue using this book's launching and consolidating learning strategies to stay focused on engagement. Return to the sections on how to reach them in each chapter. As you decide on instructional strategies to implement as a staff, make sure you

Record what mindset you think each student in your class displays. It may be helpful to have class lists available, but it is critical that you do not write students' names on this sheet. Instead, give each student an identifying number and record those instead.

Students With the:					
Agitator Mindset	Retreater Mindset	Probationer Mindset	Aficionado Mindset	Academician Mindset	

Figure 7.1: Student engagement mindset assessment.

*Visit **go.SolutionTree.com/instruction** for a free reproducible version of this figure.*

can identify how these strategies impact each of the key characteristics that build motivation. Teachers must identify how to tailor their lessons' autonomy, competence, and relatedness.

Having teachers complete the assessment is an important first step in helping them apply the information in this book. However, as mentioned earlier, *the mindsets are not labels that stay with a student* and should not be used as such. This activity reveals the different perceptions teachers have about any one student, and lets them discover how one teacher may be able to engage a particular student and help other teachers do the same. This is especially helpful in secondary schools, where a teacher can see over a hundred students in a day.

Ensure collaboration during this step. You're going to need it because the next step is a call to action that requires collective responsibility.

How Would It Feel to Be a Part of a Team That Helps Increase Student Engagement, Not Just in One Class, but Throughout a School?

Now that you know who is in the zone of critical need (and on its cusp), what are you going to do to address that problem? Ask staff if they will be part of a team that supports its members. Schools need staff to unite to overcome the gaps in achievement (Muhammad, 2009). Classroom or one grade-level or subject-area team can do this, but you can never accomplish the mission of engaging all students without all staff coming together. This means more than teachers, too. Consider the other faculty, custodians, and assistants. What are their roles in helping engage students?

All members of the school community will contribute to students' sense of affective connection to school. Collective responsibility among the staff has a statistically significant correlation to student achievement (McNeece, 2017). Working alone, the feat of engaging all students is nearly impossible.

Collective responsibility is the key to helping each other. It can be defined as when (Michigan Department of Education, n.d.):

- Instructional staff teams and individuals take active roles in creating and leading professional learning.
- Instructional staff holds one another accountable for implementing what is learned from professional learning.
- Instructional staff holds one another accountable for the improved student performance that should result from the implementation of professional learning.

Collective responsibility occurs when educators teach staff, hold each other accountable for working as a team, and look at the data related to how students have grown. That is a recipe for academic growth.

Work With Parents

Work with parents on the topic of student engagement so they can understand their role in framing their child's mindset. Engaging parents may be as difficult (or as easy) as engaging their children. Engaged parents give a child and school so many benefits. It is a worthwhile focus for the school-improvement team. Engaged parents benefit students (Harvard Family Research Project, 2006).

- Students whose parents read to them at home recognize letters of the alphabet and write their names sooner than those whose parents do not.

- Students in grades K–3 whose parents participate in school activities have high-quality work habits and task orientation.

- Students whose parents monitor their academic and social activities have lower rates of delinquency and higher rates of social competence and academic growth.

- Students whose parents are familiar with college-preparation requirements and are engaged in the application process are most likely to graduate high school and attend college.

With that said, unengaged parents give a school a golden opportunity for boosting student achievement. Consider that unengaged parents may not have had the best school experience when they were students. You may need to reach out to them multiple times through multiple methods.

Engage parents on two fronts: (1) with their child and (2) with their school community (Price-Mitchell & Grijalva, 2007). A child whose parents help him or her will display the positive outcomes described. Parent contributions to the school community are another critical engagement piece. Strong parent volunteer systems are a support for everything that a school does. Where are your students' parents in their engagement? How can you help them engage with their children's education and with their children's school community? Use your school-improvement time and strategies to help make that happen. Engaged parents lead to engaged students.

Use Student Motivation as Part of the Process

Use student motivation as part of the school-improvement and district-improvement process. Proper launching and consolidating, guided by this book's Unstoppable Learning framework and engagement solutions, will achieve this.

As you read, you learned the different ways students are motivated, and you learned how to move that motivation from extrinsic to intrinsic. Employing the various aspects and need levels for them, customized to their needs, you help develop students' sense of autonomy, competence, and relatedness (Appleton et al., 2008). If they're engaged, they're motivated.

Make sure your school-improvement meetings include conversations about these self-determination pieces. How are staff building student autonomy in their lessons? How are staff developing students' sense of competence? Finally, what are staff doing in the classrooms and the school to help kids feel a bond, to encourage relatedness?

Have Staff Model and Celebrate Lifelong Learning

Have staff demonstrate and celebrate the gift of being lifelong learners. Many times, educators will tell students that it's important to be a lifelong learner. When do students see teachers modeling that in the classroom?

Students will see the importance of building an intrinsic love for learning when the leaders of a school and the classroom celebrate that in overt ways. Talk to your students about how you are growing in your profession. What professional articles and books did you read? What data did you analyze? Principals can communicate the same thing from the office. When you talk about the vision for your school and how you want students to increase their learning, talk about how you are trying to better your understandings to serve them. What learning have you done outside of the school—as part of a graduate class or a conference, for example? Tell your teachers, staff, and students how important your learning is to the school and to yourself. Finally, consider having your teachers participate in the genius hour while your students work on their passion projects. Share the outcomes of the great new things your teachers learn.

The Galileo Institute for Teacher Leadership (https://oakland.edu/galileo) brings in teachers from all over the Detroit area for training on reflection and action research. If your school has a program like this, displaying those artifacts is a critical aspect of celebrating teachers as lifelong learners.

Allow Teacher and Student Autonomy—and Share It

Allow teachers and students a high degree of autonomy in searching out effective strategies that fit their school's goal. Autonomy should never reflect an ability to maintain the status quo. Instead teachers' creativity needs to be allowed, honored, and encouraged. The next great instructional strategies will come from teachers when they are allowed to seek out the best and most productive methods to help their students learn.

A school will never increase the amount of student learning without deviating from what has always been taught and how it has always been taught. Standards need to drive our work in the classroom, but dusting off the same lesson plan each year doesn't spur growth. Administrators should welcome and celebrate great gains when teachers demonstrate autonomy. Collaboration needs to have a special time when teachers share their methods as part of a collective inquiry of improved learning, which is also a celebration of lifelong learning. Without the sharing, those methods may stay hidden in those classes where a teacher is doing amazing work.

Teachers can use the strategies in this book, and from there, they will find more methods that positively launch and consolidate learning. If you don't share those ideas, we can never reach our mission of a school where all students learn at high levels (DuFour et al., 2016). The creative innovations to launch and consolidate learning that come from teacher autonomy must be part of collaboration.

Train, Encourage, and Monitor Instructional Strategies

Train, encourage, and monitor the use of effective instructional strategies like launching and consolidating learning. Support and accountability go hand in hand when implementing strategies that work. All teachers, administrators, and staff in a school need to be focused on learning and growing these strategies.

Teachers, do you use these strategies in your classroom? Identify in which zone of the Venn diagram in figure 1.2 (page 16) you would place each. Where do your go-to strategies fall on the diagram? Do this individually and then as a group as you develop and decide on instructional strategies.

Launching strategies from *Unstoppable Learning* (Fisher & Frey, 2015) follow.

- **Demonstrations:** This attention-grabbing introduction of a phenomenon is meant to promote high levels of interest and future inquiry into the topic.

- **Discrepant events:** This event can be staged. It is meant to challenge students' current perceptions or reality, and it creates a vulnerability that opens students to the topic.

- **Visual displays:** Many times these displays are technology based, but not always so. Students interact around an image a teacher has selected or manipulated.

- **Thought-provoking questions:** From the K-W-L to the use of provocative questions, this strategy "appeals to the emotional channels of learning" (Fisher & Frey, 2015, p. 60).

- **Direct explanation:** This approach develops higher-order-thinking skills when the teacher gives explicit information to help students understand the lesson. It is a great time to drop in a story to connect with students.

- **Modeling and think-alouds:** To develop expert thinking, the teacher verbally articulates his or her internal thoughts during a process.

- **Worked examples:** A finished problem is shown in steps where the teacher then questions and engages the students on each level of the solution.

Consolidating strategies from *Unstoppable Learning* (Fisher & Frey, 2015) follow.

- **Read-alouds:** This gives students access to a rigorous text beyond the students' comprehension, allowing for expanding knowledge beyond what was possible if they read it individually.

- **Close reading:** Reading with a pencil to follow along ends in a collaborative conversation about what students learned from the rigorous text.

- **Guest speakers:** These events help students connect with an expert's story and see how the content they are learning connects to the real world.

- **Field trips:** Students prepare, engage, and reflect on an out-of-class experience while exploring the real world.

- **Collaborative tasks:** From think-pair-share to a round table, students engage each other to explore or solidify concepts.

- **Argumentation:** Students take information or background knowledge and independently develop reasoning and logic to interact with the opposite point of view.

- **Project- or problem-based learning:** There is not a clearly defined answer or a question that is intentionally difficult to solve. Solutions are unique and independently driven by teams. The teams' personal skills are the tools that create the solution. Teams present their findings.

Administrators—what current practices do your staff use? Do you have any resident experts on great instructional practices? Set up teachers to visit those classes so they can see the engaging instruction. Learning from watching each other via instructional rounds is an excellent way to help strengthen all staff members' instruction. Next, support your teachers by providing them with the best professional development on instructional strategies. Have staff learning be part of every staff meeting, possibly by reading this book chapter by chapter during an academic school year. Talk about the mindsets at a staff meeting. Finally, model what you want in the classroom, and use launching and consolidating instructional strategies at staff meetings. When the teachers see you growing, they will look at their strategies and change to help students learn at a high level.

Finally, monitor the implementation. Be in the classrooms every day. Make sure any observations that are part of your teacher's evaluation are about growth in these skills and that they know that you know a quiet classroom is not always a learning classroom. Tell them you would rather have the instructional strategies that will help engage students rather than a so-called perfect outcome. Learning is messy. Embrace that and communicate it to your staff. Make sure teachers know that using the best instructional strategies for their students is what you want to see.

Summary

Teachers and administrators can take steps to improve student engagement. Work together as a team, using the student engagement mindsets, to develop the instructional practices your students need. Understand why you use your current methods and be open to adopting new methods. Mentally framing your work in terms of launching and consolidating learning will help you achieve your instructional goals.

Epilogue

Throughout this book, I have tried to both explain this mental model of engagement and provide practical steps to help increase student engagement. Increased engagement means higher levels of learning and, most important, developing a person's love of learning—the ultimate hope for educators. Hopefully, the described mindsets resonate with you so you can apply what you have read. The list of strategies is not exhaustive. You have instructional gifts to share.

Optimistically, Fisher and Frey's (2015) concepts of launching and consolidating, and their coordinating strategies, help you set tone and context (launching) and create situations where your students succeed (consolidating). Remember to use those launching strategies to build relatedness to the school, classmates, the content, and you, the teacher or administrator. Use the consolidating strategies to build autonomy and competence.

I hope reading this book leads you to a new mental model for how instruction and learning can happen in your classroom. It may help you to run through your thinking. Do that each time you launch a lesson for your students. You should see their engagement levels and motivation source change. Think deeply about your students' needs and go beyond the unit topic to help them build relatedness with the content, each other, and you.

As you consolidate the learning and students perform higher-order thinking, and as you build your students' levels of competence and autonomy, make sure you understand the cause and effect of your lesson's structure. The same amazing lesson won't work twice without you doing some systems thinking on the issues the students bring and need your help overcoming. Your students are different each year. Also consider how efficient the presented strategies are. Teachers cover massive amounts of content. You will never get a mile deep without the solid instructional strategies described in this book.

I promised in chapter 1 that I would finish the story that I began about my best friend Joshua. We drifted apart after he dropped out of high school, but how our paths reconnected has changed my entire perspective.

The story picks back up during my first few years of teaching. I moved from being an elementary teacher to Levey Middle School in Southfield, Michigan. There was a new principal there, Anthony Muhammad. At our very first staff meeting, he talked about the difference we make as educators. He talked about how, when we engage students in their education and when we help move a disengaged student into the engaged zone, we change lives. That success ripples throughout time, just as failure would have. We impact the life and generations of the students we change for the good.

I remember thinking about Joshua and how he disengaged. I hadn't seen or spoken to him in years. I had guilt about that; I felt like I had turned my back on my friend. Muhammad challenged us to become the best teachers in the world, and I decided to take on that challenge. I wanted to make sure not to lose any one of my students the way Joshua had been lost to his school.

Eventually, I became principal of Douglas Elementary School in Garden City, Michigan. In 2008, during my second year at Douglas, my life changed forever. It was the beginning of the school year. I was doing the morning announcements and introducing the students who were there to lead the Pledge of Allegiance. A new transfer student was among them. I began saying her name and stumbled when I realized it was my goddaughter, Ebony, I was introducing.

I was dumbfounded and awestruck. My goddaughter, whom I had not seen for ten years, was standing in front of me. Joshua and I did not grow up near Garden City. Ebony, who lived with her mom, had lived in four states in four years. She came to Douglas behind in both reading and mathematics comprehension. I believe it was divine intervention. Joshua and I were able to reconnect. To this day, we've stayed close. He earned his GED and married a wonderful woman, who is a teacher. In 2016, we celebrated Ebony's high school graduation. She is studying to be a nurse. With the help of many people who loved her, she broke the cycle of disengagement.

I tell this story to let educators know the difference they make and that I do not believe in chance. I believe you are reading this book for a reason. I believe you are empowered with understanding and language to help increase engagement. When you take a student with the agitator, retreater, or probationer mindset and increase his or her engagement, you create positive and tangible results in that student's life now, tomorrow, and for years to come. When you help a student with an aficionado mindset gain an intrinsic love for learning, you'll see limitless results. When you challenge a student with the academician mindset, you can push them to do amazing things that change the world. Increased engagement ripples through generations. The positive difference you make is immense.

References and Resources

academician. (n.d.). In *Oxford English Dictionary Online*. Accessed at www.oed.com on December 31, 2017.

Adelman, H. S., & Taylor, L. (2006). *The school leader's guide to student learning supports: New directions for addressing barriers to learning*. Thousand Oaks, CA: SAGE.

aficionado. (n.d.). In *Oxford English Dictionary Online*. Accessed at www.oed.com on December 31, 2017.

Ahlum-Heath, M. E., & Di Vesta, F. J. (1986). The effect of conscious controlled verbalization of a cognitive strategy on transfer in problem solving. *Memory and Cognition, 14*(3), 281–285.

Ainley, M. (2004). *What do we know about student motivation and engagement?* Paper presented at the annual meeting of the Australian Association for Research in Education, Melbourne. Accessed at www.aare.edu.au/data/publications/2004/ain04760.pdf on March 29, 2018.

Alexie, S. (2007). *The absolutely true diary of a part-time Indian*. Boston: Little, Brown.

Alliance for Excellent Education. (2003a). *FactSheet: The impact of education on—Crime*. Washington, DC: Author.

Alliance for Excellent Education. (2003b). *FactSheet: The impact of education on—The economy*. Washington, DC: Author.

Alpert, B. (1991). Students' resistance in the classroom. *Anthropology and Education Quarterly, 22*(4), 350–366.

Altenbaugh, R. J. (1998). "Some teachers are ignorant": Teachers and teaching through urban school leavers' eyes. In B. M. Franklin (Ed.), *When children don't learn: Student failure and the culture of teaching* (pp. 52–71). New York: Teachers College Press.

American Psychiatric Association. (2013). *Diagnostic and statistical manual of mental disorders (DSM-5)*. (5th ed.). Arlington, VA: Author.

Angelou, M. (2002). *I know why the caged bird sings*. New York: Random House.

Appleton, J. J., Christenson, S. L., & Furlong, M. J. (2008). Student engagement with school: Critical conceptual and methodological issues of the construct. *Psychology in the Schools, 45*(5), 369–386.

Arnstein, S. R. (1969). A ladder of citizen participation. *Journal of the American Institute of Planners, 35*(4), 216–224.

Bain, K. (2004). *What the best college teachers do.* Cambridge, MA: Harvard University Press.

Bandura, A. (1997). *Self-efficacy: The exercise of control.* New York: Freeman.

Barlow, D. H. (2004). *Anxiety and its disorders: The nature and treatment of anxiety and panic* (2nd ed.). New York: Guilford Press.

Baumeister, R. F., & Leary, M. R. (1995). The need to belong: Desire for interpersonal attachments as a fundamental human motivation. *Psychological Bulletin, 117*(3), 497–529.

Beard, K. S. (2015). Theoretically speaking: An interview with Mihaly Csikszentmihalyi on flow theory development and its usefulness in addressing contemporary challenges in education. *Educational Psychology Review, 27*(2), 353–364. Accessed at https://doi.org/10.1007/s10648 –014–9291–1 on March 29, 2018.

Belfield, C. R., Levin, H. M., & Rosen, R. (2012). *The economic value of opportunity youth.* Washington, DC: Corporation for National and Community Service.

Bell, H., Limberg, D., & Robinson, E. (2013). Recognizing trauma in the classroom: A practical guide for educators. *Childhood Education, 89*(3), 139–145.

Berman, M. L. (2002). Are you a seeker or an avoider? You can change avoidance behaviors; trainers play a crucial role. *Talent Development, 56*(12), 38–42.

Betts, J. R., & Shkolnik, J. L. (2000). The effects of ability grouping on student achievement and resource allocation in secondary schools. *Economics of Education Review, 19*(1), 1–15.

Black, A. E., & Deci, E. L. (2000). The effects of instructors' autonomy support and students' autonomous motivation on learning organic chemistry: A self-determination theory perspective. *Science Education, 84*(6), 740–756.

Black, P., & Wiliam, D. (2018, March 22). Classroom assessment and pedagogy. *Assessment in Education: Principles, Policy & Practice, 25*(3). Accessed at www.tandfonline.com/doi/full/10 .1080/0969594X.2018.1441807 on October 16, 2018.

Black, S. (2004). Teachers CAN engage disengaged students. *Education Digest: Essential Readings Condensed for Quick Review, 69*(7), 39–44.

Borg, M. (2004). The apprenticeship of observation. *ELT Journal, 58*(3), 274–276.

Brail, S. (2016). Quantifying the value of service-learning: A comparison of grade achievement between service-learning and non-service-learning students. *International Journal of Teaching and Learning in Higher Education, 28*(2), 148–157.

Brizio, A., Gabbatore, I., Tirassa, M., & Bosco, F. M. (2015). "No more a child, not yet an adult": Studying social cognition in adolescence. Accessed at www.frontiersin.org/articles /10.3389/fpsyg.2015.01011/full on August 23, 2018.

Brookfield, S. D. (2006). *The skillful teacher: On technique, trust, and responsiveness in the classroom.* San Francisco: Jossey-Bass.

Brown, B. B., & Larson, J. (2009). Peer relationships in adolescence. In R. M. Lerner & L. Steinberg (Eds.), *Handbook of adolescent psychology, volume 2: Contextual influences on adolescent development* (3rd ed., pp. 74–103). Hoboken, NJ: Wiley.

Buckner, E., Shores, M., Sloane, M., Dantzler, J., Shields, C., Shader, K., et al. (2016). Honors and non-honors student engagement: A model of student, curricular, and institutional characteristics. *Journal of the National Collegiate Honors Council, 17*(1), 191–217.

Burgess, D. (2012). *Teach like a pirate: Increase student engagement, boost your creativity, and transform your life as an educator*. San Diego, CA: Burgess Consulting.

Cacioppo, J. T., & Hawkley, L. C. (2009). Loneliness. In M. R. Leary & R. H. Hoyle (Eds.), *Handbook of individual differences in social behavior* (pp. 227–240). New York: Guilford Press.

Cairns, R. B., & Cairns, B. D. (1994). *Lifelines and risks: Pathways of youth in our time*. Cambridge, England: Cambridge University Press.

Cannon, W. B. (1932). *The wisdom of the body*. New York: Norton.

Carlton, M. P., & Winsler, A. (1998). Fostering intrinsic motivation in early childhood classrooms. *Early Childhood Education Journal, 25*(3), 159–166.

Carpenter, J. J. (2004). Jefferson's views on education: Implications for today's social studies. *Social Studies, 95*(4), 140–146.

Catterall, J. S. (1985). *On the social costs of dropping out of schools* (Report No. 86-SEPT-3). Stanford, CA: Center for Educational Research.

Center on the Developing Child. (n.d.). *Resilience*. Accessed at https://developingchild.harvard.edu/science/key-concepts/resilience on February 6, 2018.

Centers for Disease Control and Prevention. (n.d.). *Characteristics of an effective health education curriculum*. Accessed at www.cdc.gov/healthyschools/sher/characteristics/index.htm on August 23, 2018.

Clarke, M. (2011). Promoting a culture of reflection in teacher education: The challenge of large lecture settings. *Teacher Development, 15*(4), 517–531.

Clifford, M. M. (1988). Failure tolerance and academic risk-taking in ten- to twelve-year-old students. *British Journal of Educational Psychology, 58*(1), 15–27.

Clifford, M. M. (1991). Risk taking: Theoretical, empirical, and educational considerations. *Educational Psychologist, 26*(3–4), 263–297.

Collins, C. (2015, October 6). For kids, living in poverty is living with chronic trauma, experts say. *KERA News*. Accessed at http://keranews.org/post/kids-living-poverty-living-chronic-trauma-experts-say on March 8, 2018.

context. (n.d.). In *Merriam-Webster's online dictionary*. Accessed at www.merriam-webster.com/dictionary/context on December 31, 2017.

Cothran, D. J., & Ennis, C. D. (2000). Building bridges to student engagement: Communicating respect and care for students in urban high schools. *Journal of Research and Development in Education, 33*(2), 106–117.

Covington, M. V. (2000). Intrinsic versus extrinsic motivation in schools: A reconciliation. *Current Directions in Psychological Science, 9*(1), 22–25.

Cross, J. R., O'Reilly, C., Kim, M., Mammadov, S., & Cross, T. L. (2015). Social coping and self-concept among young gifted students in Ireland and the United States: A cross-cultural study. *High Ability Studies, 26*(1), 39–61.

Csikszentmihalyi, M. (1990). *Flow: The psychology of optimal experience*. New York: Harper & Row.

Csikszentmihalyi, M. (2008). *Flow: The psychology of optimal experience*. New York: Harper Perennial.

Darr, C. W. (2012). Measuring student engagement: The development of a scale for formative use. In S. L. Christenson, A. L. Reschly, & C. Wylie (Eds.), *Handbook of research on student engagement* (pp. 707–723). New York: Springer.

Davenport, M. (2016, September 22). *Socratic seminars: Building a culture of student-led discussion* [Blog post]. Accessed at www.edutopia.org/blog/socratic-seminars-culture-student-led -discussion-mary-davenport on March 29, 2018.

Davidson, A. J., Gest, S. D., & Welsh, J. A. (2010). Relatedness with teachers and peers during early adolescence: An integrated variable-oriented and person-oriented approach. *Journal of School Psychology, 48*(6), 483–510.

de Boer, H., Bosker, R. J., & Van der Werf, M. P. C. (2010). Sustainability of teacher expectation bias effects on long-term student performance. *Journal of Educational Psychology, 102*(1), 168–179.

Deci, E. L., Koestner, R., & Ryan, R. M. (1999). A meta-analytic review of experiments examining the effects of extrinsic rewards on intrinsic motivation. *Psychological Bulletin, 125*(6), 627–668. Accessed at http://dx.doi.org/10.1037/0033–2909.125.6.627 on March 29, 2018.

Deci, E. L., & Ryan, R. M. (2002). *Intrinsic motivation and self-determination in human behavior.* New York: Plenum Press.

Deci, E. L., & Ryan, R. M. (2008a). Self-determination theory: A macrotheory of human motivation, development, and health. *Canadian Psychology, 49*(3), 182–185.

Deci, E. L., & Ryan, R. M. (2008b). Facilitating optimal motivation and psychological well-being across life's domains. *Canadian Psychology, 49*(1), 14–23.

Deci, E. L., & Ryan, R. M. (2014). Autonomy and need satisfaction in close relationships: Relationships motivation theory. In N. Weinstein (Ed.), *Human motivation and interpersonal relationships: Theory, research, and applications* (pp. 53–73). Dordrecht, the Netherlands: Springer.

Deed, C. G. (2008a). Bending the school rules to re-engage students: Implications for improving teaching practice. *Improving Schools, 11*(3), 205–212.

Deed, C. G. (2008b). Disengaged boys' perspectives about learning. *Education 3–13, 36*(1), 3–14. Accessed at http://dx.doi.org/10.1080/03004270701577248 on March 29, 2018.

Depka, E. (2017). *Raising the rigor: Effective questioning strategies and techniques for the classroom.* Bloomington, IN: Solution Tree Press.

Ditkoff, M. (2011, December 16). *The heart of innovation: The Atlassian FedEx Day goes global* [Blog post]. Accessed at www.ideachampions.com/weblogs/archives/2011/12/atlassian_is_a.shtml on August 1, 2018.

Dockterman, E. (2013, November 15). *Candy Crush Saga*: The science behind our addiction. *TIME.* Accessed at http://business.time.com/2013/11/15/candy-crush-saga-the-science-behind -our-addiction on March 29, 2018.

Duda, J. L., & Nicholls, J. G. (1992). Dimensions of achievement motivation in schoolwork and sport. *Journal of Educational Psychology, 84*(3), 290–299.

DuFour, R. (2012). *Implementing the PLC process: Will you soar or settle?* Presented at the Professional Learning Communities at Work Institute, Phoenix, AZ.

DuFour, R., DuFour, R., Eaker, R., Many, T. W., & Mattos, M. (2016). *Learning by doing: A handbook for Professional Learning Communities at Work* (3rd ed.). Bloomington, IN: Solution Tree Press.

DuFour, R., DuFour, R., Lopez, D., & Muhammad, A. (2006). Promises kept: Collective commitments to students become a catalyst for improved professional practice. *Journal of Staff Development, 27*(3), 53–56.

DuFour, R., & Eaker, R. (1998). *Professional Learning Communities at Work: Best practices for enhancing student achievement.* Bloomington, IN: Solution Tree Press.

Durden, T. (2011). *Making it happen: Building positive relationships with children. HEF601 participant guide.* Accessed at http://digitalcommons.unl.edu/cgi/viewcontent.cgi?article =1042&context=cyfsfacpub on October 17, 2018.

Dweck, C. S. (2006). *Mindset: The new psychology of success.* New York: Ballantine Books.

Estell, D. B., Farmer, T. W., & Cairns, B. D. (2007). Bullies and victims in rural African American youth: Behavioral characteristics and social network placement. *Aggressive Behavior, 33*(2), 145–159.

Farmer, T. W., Hall, C. M., Weiss, M. P., Petrin, R. A., Meece, J. L., & Moohr, M. (2011). The school adjustment of rural adolescents with and without disabilities: Variable and person-centered approaches. *Journal of Child and Family Studies, 20*(1), 78–88. Accessed at http://dx.doi.org/10.1007/s10826-010-9379-2 on March 29, 2018.

Festinger, L. (1957). *A theory of cognitive dissonance.* Redwood City, CA: Stanford University Press.

Fisher, D. (2008). *Effective use of the gradual release of responsibility model.* Accessed at www.researchgate.net/publication/266351394_Effective_Use_of_the_Gradual_Release_of_Responsibility_Model_The_Gradual_Release_of_Responsibility_Model on July 10, 2018.

Fisher, D., & Frey, N. (2008). *Better learning through structured teaching: A framework for the gradual release of responsibility.* Alexandria, VA: Association for Supervision and Curriculum Development.

Fisher, D., & Frey, N. (2014). Student and teacher perspectives on a close reading protocol. *Literacy Research and Instruction, 53*(1), 25–49.

Fisher, D., & Frey, N. (2015). *Unstoppable learning: Seven essential elements to unleash student potential.* Bloomington, IN: Solution Tree Press.

Fisher, D., Frey, N., & Hattie, J. (2016). *Visible learning for literacy, grades K–12: Implementing the practices that work best to accelerate student learning.* Thousand Oaks, CA: Corwin Press.

Fisher, D., Frey, N., & Lapp, D. (2011). Focusing on the participation and engagement gap: A case study on closing the achievement gap. *Journal of Education for Students Placed at Risk, 16*(1), 56–64.

Fredricks, J., McColskey, W., Meli, J., Mordica, J., Montrosse, B., & Mooney, K. (2011). *Measuring student engagement in upper elementary through high school: A description of 21 instruments* (Issues & Answers, REL 2011–No. 098). Washington, DC: Institute of Education Sciences, National Center for Education Evaluation and Regional Assistance. Accessed at https://ies.ed.gov /ncee/edlabs/regions/southeast/pdf/REL_2011098.pdf on May 21, 2018.

Fredricks, J. A., Blumenfeld, P. C., & Paris, A. H. (2004). School engagement: Potential of the concept, state of the evidence. *Review of Educational Research, 74*(1), 59–109.

Friedrich, A., Flunger, B., Nagengast, B., Jonkmann, K., & Trautwein, U. (2015). Pygmalion effects in the classroom: Teacher expectancy effects on students' math achievement. *Contemporary Educational Psychology, 41*, 1–12.

Furlong, M. J., & Christenson, S. L. (2008). Engaging students at school and with learning: A relevant construct for *all* students. *Psychology in the Schools, 45*(5), 365–368.

Furrer, C., & Skinner, E. (2003). Sense of relatedness as a factor in children's academic engagement and performance. *Journal of Educational Psychology, 95*(1), 148–162.

Gladwell, M. (2005). *Blink: The power of thinking without thinking.* New York: Little, Brown.

Grant, M., Lapp, D., Fisher, D., Johnson, K., & Frey, N. (2012). Purposeful instruction: Mixing up the "I," "we," and "you." *Journal of Adolescent & Adult Literacy, 56*(1), 45–55.

Gunderson, J. A. (2003). *Csikszentmihalyi's state of flow and effective teaching.* Unpublished doctoral dissertation, Claremont Graduate University, California.

Guskey, T. R. (2007). Leadership in the age of accountability. *Educational Horizons, 86*(1), 29–34.

Guthrie, J. T., & Wigfield, A. (2000). Engagement and motivation in reading. In M. L. Kamil, P. B. Mosenthal, P. D. Pearson, & R. Barr (Eds.), *Handbook of reading research* (Vol. 3, pp. 403–422). Mahwah, NJ: Lawrence Erlbaum.

Gwyn, L. P. (2004). *Sustained engagement in mathematics for elementary school learners: A narrative study of the relationship between classroom practices and incidence of flow learning situations for third- and fifth-grade gifted mathematics learners, or, traveling from vegemite to gorilla.* Unpublished doctoral dissertation, University of Hong Kong.

Haft, S. (Producer), Henderson, D. (Producer), Witt, P. J. (Producer), Thomas, T. (Producer), & Weir, P. (Director). (1989). *Dead poets society* [Motion picture]. United States: Touchstone Pictures.

Haley, A. (1977). *Roots: The saga of an American family.* London: Picador.

Hargreaves, A. (2010). Presentism, individualism, and conservatism: The legacy of Dan Lortie's *Schoolteacher: A Sociological Study. Curriculum Inquiry, 40*(1), 143–154. Accessed at https:// onlinelibrary.wiley.com/doi/abs/10.1111/j.1467–873X.2009.00472.x on May 25, 2018.

Harlacher, J. E., & Rodriguez, B. J. (2018). *An educator's guide to schoolwide positive behavioral interventions and supports: Integrating all three tiers.* Bloomington, IN: Marzano Research.

Harper, S. R., & Hurtado, S. (2007). Nine themes in campus racial climates and implications for institutional transformation. *New Directions for Student Services, 120*, 7–24.

Hart, R. A. (1992). *Children's participation: From tokenism to citizenship.* Florence, Italy: UNICEF International Child Development Centre. Accessed at www.unicef-irc.org/publications/pdf/childrens_participation.pdf on March 29, 2018.

Harvard Family Research Project. (2006). *Family involvement in early childhood education.* Accessed at http://5c2cabd466efc6790a0a-6728e7c952118b70f16620a9fc754159.r37.cf1.rackcdn.com/cms/Section3_1513.pdf on September 10, 2018.

Hattie, J. (2012). *Visible learning for teachers: Maximizing impact on learning.* London: Routledge.

Heick, T. (2018, April 4). *6 principles of genius hour in the classroom.* Accessed at www.teachthought.com/learning/6-principles-of-genius-hour-in-the-classroom on August 1, 2018.

Hierck, T., & Freese, A. (2018). *Assessing unstoppable learning.* Bloomington, IN: Solution Tree Press.

Holmes, P. (2012). A Nation at Risk *and education reform: A frame analysis.* Unpublished master's thesis, University of Washington, Seattle.

Jensen, E. (2013). How poverty affects classroom engagement. *Faces of Poverty, 70*(8), 24–30. Accessed at www.ascd.org/publications/educational-leadership/may13/vol70/num08/How-Poverty-Affects-Classroom-Engagement.aspx on August 17, 2018.

Jensen, E. (2016). *Poor students, rich teaching: Mindsets for change.* Bloomington, IN: Solution Tree Press.

Karier, C. J. (1991). *The individual, society, and education: A history of American educational ideas* (2nd ed.). Champaign: University of Illinois Press.

Klem, A. M., & Connell, J. P. (2004). Relationships matter: Linking teacher support to student engagement and achievement. *Journal of School Health, 74*(7), 262–273. Accessed at https://onlinelibrary.wiley.com/doi/pdf/10.1111/j.1746–1561.2004.tb08283.x on May 3, 2018.

Koebler, J. (2011, June 13). National high school graduation rates improve. *U.S. News & World Report.* Accessed at www.usnews.com/education/blogs/high-school-notes/2011/06/13/national-high-school-graduation-rates-improve on March 29, 2018.

Kohn, A. (1994). *The risks of rewards.* Accessed at https://eric.ed.gov/?id=ED376990 on March 29, 2018.

Kohn, A. (2016, December 12). *The case for abolishing class rank* [Blog post]. Accessed at www.alfiekohn.org/blogs/class-rank on August 23, 2018.

Krajcik, J. S., & Blumenfeld, P. C. (2006). Project-based learning. In R. K. Sawyer (Ed.), *The Cambridge handbook of the learning sciences* (pp. 317–334). New York: Cambridge University Press.

Kunter, M., Tsai, Y-M., Klusmann, U., Brunner, M., Krauss, S., & Baumert, J. (2008). Students' and mathematics teachers' perceptions of teacher enthusiasm and instruction. *Learning and Instruction, 18*(5), 468–482.

Kuzhabekova, A., & Zhaparova, R. (2016). The effects of apprenticeship of observation on teachers' attitudes towards active learning instruction. *Educational Studies, 2,* 208–228.

Lease, A. M., Kennedy, C. A., & Axelrod, J. L. (2002). Children's social constructions of popularity. *Social Development, 11*(1), 87–109.

Legault, L., Green-Demers, I., & Pelletier, L. (2006). Why do high school students lack motivation in the classroom? Toward an understanding of academic amotivation and the role of social support. *Journal of Educational Psychology*, *98*(3), 567–582.

Levin, H. M., Belfield, C., Muennig, P. A., & Rouse, C. (2007). The public returns to public educational investments in African-American males. *Economics of Education Review*, *26*(6), 699–708.

Liu, N-F., & Carless, D. (2006). Peer feedback: The learning element of peer assessment. *Teaching in Higher Education*, *11*(3), 279–290.

Livdahl, B. J. (1991). The learner-centered classroom: Explorations into language and learning. *Insights into Open Education*, *24*(1), 2–10.

Lleras, C., & Rangel, C. (2009). Ability grouping practices in elementary school and African American/Hispanic achievement. *American Journal of Education*, *115*(2), 279–304.

Lortie, D. C. (1975). *Schoolteacher: A sociological study*. Chicago: University of Chicago Press.

Loveless, T. (2013). *The 2013 Brown Center Report on American Education: How well are American students learning?* Washington, DC: Brown Center on Education Policy at Brookings. Accessed at www.brookings.edu/research/the-resurgence-of-ability -grouping-and-persistence-of-tracking on May 4, 2018.

Lowry, L. (1989). *Number the stars*. Boston: Houghton Mifflin Harcourt.

Malloy, J. A., Parsons, S. A., & Parsons, A. W. (2013). Methods for evaluating literacy engagement as a fluid construct. *Literacy Research Association Yearbook*, *62*, 124–139.

Mason, C., Rivers Murphy, M. M., & Jackson, Y. (2019). *Mindfulness practices: Cultivating heart centered communities where students focus and flourish*. Bloomington, IN: Solution Tree Press.

Matera, B. D. (2009). *The effects of rewards and punishments on motivations of the elementary school student*. Unpublished doctoral dissertation, Walden University, Minneapolis, Minnesota.

Mazer, J. P. (2012). Development and validation of the student interest and engagement scales. *Journal of Communication Methods and Measures*, *6*(2), 99–125.

McNeece, A. A. (2017). *Michigan's quantitative school culture inventories and student achievement*. Unpublished doctoral dissertation, Eastern Michigan University, Ypsilanti.

McRaney, D. (2011). *The backfire effect*. Accessed at https://youarenotsosmart.com/2011/06/10/the -backfire-effect on May 24, 2018.

Melville, H. (1851). *Moby-Dick; or, The Whale*. New York: Harper & Brothers.

Meyer, D. K., Turner, J. C., & Spencer, C. A. (1997). Challenge in a mathematics classroom: Students' motivation and strategies in project-based learning. *The Elementary School Journal*, *97*(5), 501–521. Accessed at www.jstor.org/stable/1002266 on March 29, 2018.

Michigan Department of Education. (n.d.). *Resources for conducting a school systems review*. Accessed at www.michigan.gov/mde/0,4615,7-140-81376_38959-346009--,00.html on August 26, 2018.

Migala, J. (2015, April 6). *This is your brain on Candy Crush Saga*. Accessed at www .womenshealthmag.com/health/a19910448/candy-crush-saga-addiction on August 16, 2018.

Miller, R. T., Murnane, R. J., & Willett, J. B. (2008). Do teacher absences impact student achievement? Longitudinal evidence from one urban school district. *Educational Evaluation and Policy Analysis, 30*(2), 181–200.

Molineux, J. (2013). Enabling organisational cultural change using systemic strategic human resource management: A longitudinal case study. *International Journal of Human Resource Management, 24*(8), 1588–1612.

Mosher, R., & MacGowan, B. (1985). *Assessing student engagement in secondary schools: Alternative conceptions, strategies of assessing, and instruments.* Madison: University of Wisconsin Research and Development Center.

Muhammad, A. (2009). *Transforming school culture: How to overcome staff division.* Bloomington, IN: Solution Tree Press.

Muhammad, A. (2015). *Overcoming the achievement gap trap: Liberating mindsets to effect change.* Bloomington, IN: Solution Tree Press.

Muhammad, A. (2018). *Transforming school culture: How to overcome staff division* (2nd ed.). Bloomington, IN: Solution Tree Press.

National Center for Education Statistics. (2001). *Dropout rates in the United States: 2000.* Washington, DC: Author. Accessed at http://nces.ed.gov/pubsearch/pubsinfo.asp ?pubid=2002114 on March 29, 2018.

National Center for Education Statistics. (2002). *Education longitudinal study of 2002.* Accessed at https://nces.ed.gov/surveys/ELS2002 on May 5, 2018.

National Center for Education Statistics. (2013). *The condition of education 2013.* Accessed at https://nces.ed.gov/pubs2013/2013037.pdf on May 17, 2018.

National Dropout Prevention Center. (n.d.). *Economic impacts of dropouts.* Accessed at http:// dropoutprevention.org/resources/statistics/quick-facts/economic-impacts-of-dropouts on December 31, 2017.

National Research Council. (2011). *High school dropout, graduation, and completion rates: Better data, better measures, better decisions.* Washington, DC: National Academies Press.

No Child Left Behind Act of 2001, 20 U.S.C.A. § 6301 (2002).

Noddings, N. (2006). *Critical lessons: What our schools should teach.* New York: Cambridge University Press.

Ormrod, J. E. (2003). *Educational psychology: Developing learners* (4th ed). Upper Saddle River, NJ: Merrill Prentice Hall.

Pajares, F. (2003). Self-efficacy beliefs, motivation, and achievement in writing: A review of the literature. *Reading and Writing Quarterly, 19*(2), 139–158.

Pajares, F., & Schunk, D. H. (2002). Self and self-belief in psychology and education: A historical perspective. In J. Aronson (Ed.), *Improving academic achievement: Impact of psychological factors on education* (pp. 3–21). San Diego, CA: Academic Press.

Palardy, J. M. (1988). The effect of homework policies on student achievement. *NASSP Bulletin, 72*(507), 14–17.

Parish, P. (1963). *Amelia Bedelia.* New York: Harper & Row.

Parsons, S. A., Nuland, L. R., & Parsons, A. W. (2014). The ABCs of student engagement. *Phi Delta Kappan*, *95*(8), 23–27.

Perry, N. E., Turner, J. C., & Meyer, D. K. (2006). Classrooms as contexts for motivating learning. In P. A. Alexander & P. H. Winne (Eds.), *Handbook of educational psychology* (2nd ed., pp. 327–348). New York: Routledge.

Piaget, J. (1926). *The language and thought of the child*. Paris: Routledge & Kegan Paul.

Pink, D. H. (2009). *Drive: The surprising truth about what motivates us*. New York: Riverhead Books.

Price-Mitchell, M., & Grijalva, S. (2007). *Children have the POTENTIAL to achieve their dreams: An introductory guide for parent leaders, educators and trainers*. Accessed at www.wafamily engagement.org/system_files/library/102.pdf on September 10, 2018.

probation. (n.d.). In *Oxford English Dictionary Online*. Accessed at www.oed.com on March 29, 2018.

probationer. (n.d.). In *Oxford English Dictionary Online*. Accessed at www.oed.com on March 29, 2018.

Reynolds, C. R., & Kamphaus, R. W. (2013). *BASC3*. Accessed at https://images.pearsonclinical .com/images/assets/basc-3/basc3resources/DSM5_DiagnosticCriteria_MajorDepressiveDisorder .pdf on March 29, 2018.

Rich, M., Cox, A., & Bloch, M. (2016, April 29). Money, race and success: How your school district compares. *The New York Times*. Accessed at www.nytimes.com/interactive/2016/04/29 /upshot/money-race-and-success-how-your-school-district-compares.html?_r=1 on March 29, 2018.

Rimm-Kaufman, S. E., Baroody, A. E., Larsen, R. A. A., Curby, T. W., & Abry, T. (2015). To what extent do teacher-student interaction quality and student gender contribute to fifth graders' engagement in mathematics learning? *Journal of Educational Psychology*, *107*(1), 170–185.

Rimm-Kaufman, S. E., & Sandilos, L. (n.d.). *Improving students' relationships with teachers to provide essential supports for learning*. Accessed at www.apa.org/education/k12/relationships.aspx on May 3, 2018.

Riordan, G. (2006). Reducing student 'suspension rates' and engaging students in learning: Principal and teacher approaches that work. *Improving Schools*, *9*(3), 239–250.

Ritchhart, R. (2002). *Intellectual character: What it is, why it matters, and how to get it*. San Francisco: Jossey-Bass.

Roberson, R. (2013, September). *Helping students find relevance*. Accessed at www.apa.org/ed /precollege/ptn/2013/09/students-relevance.aspx on August 26, 2018.

Robinson, K. (2009). *The element: How finding your passion changes everything*. New York: Penguin Books.

Rodkin, P. C., Ryan, A. M., Jamison, R., & Wilson, T. (2013). Social goals, social behavior, and social status in middle childhood. *Developmental Psychology*, *49*(6), 1139–1150.

Rolland, R. G. (2012). Synthesizing the evidence on classroom goal structures in middle and secondary schools: A meta-analysis and narrative review. *Review of Educational Research*, *82*(4), 396–435.

Rosch, E. H. (1973). Natural categories. *Cognitive Psychology, 4*(3), 328–350.

Rowling, J. K. (2009). *Harry Potter: The complete series.* New York: Arthur A. Levine Books.

Rumberger, R. W. (2011). *Dropping out: Why students drop out of high school and what can be done about it.* Cambridge, MA: Harvard University Press.

Ryan, J. B., Pierce, C. D., & Mooney, P. (2008). *Evidence-based teaching strategies for students with EBD.* Accessed at www.mona.uwi.edu/cop/sites/default/files/resource/files/evidenced%20based%20teachins%20strategies%20-EDC.pdf on May 22, 2018.

Ryan, R. M., & Deci, E. L. (2000a). Intrinsic and extrinsic motivations: Classic definitions and new directions. *Contemporary Educational Psychology, 25,* 54–67.

Ryan, R. M., & Deci, E. L. (2000b). Self-determination theory and the facilitation of intrinsic motivation, social development, and well-being. *American Psychologist, 55*(1), 68–78.

Ryan, R. M., & Deci, E. L. (2009). Promoting self-determined school engagement: Motivation, learning, and well-being. In K. R. Wentzel & A. Wigfield (Eds.), *Handbook of motivation at school* (pp. 171–196). New York: Routledge.

Saeed, S., & Zyngier, D. (2012). How motivation influences student engagement: A qualitative case study. *Journal of Education and Learning, 1*(2), 252–267.

Safir, S. (2016, March 14). *5 keys to challenging implicit bias* [Blog post]. Accessed at www.edutopia.org/blog/keys-to-challenging-implicit-bias-shane-safir on May 17, 2018.

Sammons, L. R., & Smith, N. N. (2017). *A handbook for unstoppable learning.* Bloomington, IN: Solution Tree Press.

Sastry, M. A. (1997.) Problems and paradoxes in a model of punctuated organizational change. *Administrative Science Quarterly, 42*(2), 237–275.

Schein, E. H. (2004). *Organizational culture and leadership* (3rd ed.). San Francisco: Jossey-Bass.

Schempp, P. G. (1987, April). *A study of Lortie's "Apprenticeship-of-Observation" theory in physical education.* Paper presented at the annual meeting of the American Educational Research Association, Washington, DC.

Schlechty, P. C. (2001). *Shaking up the schoolhouse: How to support and sustain educational innovation.* San Francisco: Jossey-Bass.

Schussler, D. L. (2009). Beyond content: How teachers manage classrooms to facilitate intellectual engagement for disengaged students. *Theory Into Practice, 48*(2), 114–121.

Schuyler Center for Analysis and Advocacy. (2008). *Teenage births: Outcomes for young parents and their children.* Accessed at www.scaany.org/documents/teen_pregnancy_dec08.pdf on March 29, 2018.

Sedlak, M., Wheeler, C. W., Pullin, D. C., & Cusick, P. A. (1986). *Selling students short: Classroom bargains and academic reform in the American high school.* New York: Teachers College Press

Seligman, M. E. P., & Csikszentmihalyi, M. (2000). Positive psychology: An introduction. *American Psychologist, 55*(1), 5–14.

Shakespeare, W. (1973). Romeo and Juliet. In G. B. Evans , H. Levin, H. Baker, A. Barton, F. Kermode, H. Smith, M. Edel, & C. H. Shattuck (Eds.), *The Riverside Shakespeare*. Boston: Houghton Mifflin.

Shifrer, D., Muller, C., & Callahan, R. (2011). Disproportionality and learning disabilities: Parsing apart race, socioeconomic status, and language. *Journal of Learning Disabilities, 44*(3), 246–257.

Silk, J. S., Stroud, L. R., Siegle, G. J., Dahl, R. E., Lee, K. H., & Nelson, E. E. (2012). Peer acceptance and rejection through the eyes of youth: Pupillary, eyetracking and ecological data from the Chatroom Interact task. *Social Cognitive and Affective Neuroscience, 7*(1), 93–105.

Sinclair, M. F., Christenson, S. L., Lehr, C. A., & Anderson, A. R. (2003). Facilitating student engagement: Lessons learned from check and connect longitudinal studies. *California School Psychologist, 8*, 29–41.

Sizer, T. R., & Sizer, N. F. (1999). *The students are watching: Schools and the moral contract*. Boston: Beacon Press.

Skinner, R., & Chapman, C. (1999). *Service-learning and community service in K–12 public schools*. Washington, DC: National Center for Education Statistics. Accessed at https://nces.ed.gov /pubs99/1999043.pdf on August 16, 2018.

Skinner, E. A., Kindermann, T. A., & Furrer, C. J. (2009). A motivational perspective on engagement and disaffection: Conceptualization and assessment of children's behavioral and emotional participation in academic activities in the classroom. *Educational and Psychological Measurement, 69*(3), 493–525.

Skinner, E. A., & Pitzer, J. R. (2012). Developmental dynamics of student engagement, coping, and everyday resilience. In S. L. Christenson, A. L. Reschly, & C. Wylie (Eds.), *Handbook of research on student engagement*. New York: Springer.

Smith, M. (2017, September 15). *Genius hour in elementary school*. Accessed at www.edutopia.org /article/genius-hour-elementary-school on August 1, 2018.

Snyder, S. J. (2012). *Overcoming non-academic issues to gain admission into competitive entry college majors: The power of positive psychological development*. Unpublished doctoral dissertation, Western Michigan University, Kalamazoo.

Statistics Canada. (2015). *Table A.11: Graduation rate, Canada, provinces and territories, 2005/2006 to 2009/2010*. Accessed at www150.statcan.gc.ca/n1/pub/81-595-m/2011095/tbl /tbla.11-eng.htm on August 26, 2018.

Stinson, R. L. (2017). *Leading unstoppable learning*. Bloomington, IN: Solution Tree Press.

Susman, E. J., & Rogol, A. (2004). Puberty and psychological development. In R. M. Lerner & L. Steinberg (Eds.) *Handbook of adolescent psychology* (2nd ed., pp. 15–44). Hoboken, NJ: Wiley.

Tate, M. L. (2016). *Worksheets don't grow dendrites: 20 instructional strategies that engage the brain* (3rd ed.). Thousand Oaks, CA: Corwin Press.

Thomas, J. W. (2000). *A review of research on project-based learning* [White paper]. Accessed at www .bie.org/images/uploads/general/9d06758fd346969cb63653d00dca55c0.pdf on March 29, 2018.

Thompson, F., & Logue, S. (2006). An exploration of common student misconceptions in science. *International Education Journal, 7*(4), 553–559.

Tierney, W. G. (2006). The changing nature of organizational leadership and culture in academic work. *Journal of Research on Leadership Education, 1*(1), 1–3.

Tomlinson, P. (1999). Conscious reflection and implicit learning in teacher preparation. Part II: Implications for a balanced approach. *Oxford Review of Education, 25*(4), 533–544. doi:10.1080/030549899103973

University of Georgia College of Education. (n.d.). *Are your students taking risks in their learning?* Accessed at http://gca.coe.uga.edu/are-your-students-taking-risks-in-their-learning on August 24, 2018.

U.S. Department of Education Office for Civil Rights. (2014). *Civil rights data collection: Data snapshot—School discipline*. Accessed at https://ocrdata.ed.gov/downloads/crdc-school -discipline-snapshot.pdf on March 29, 2018.

U.S. Government Accountability Office. (2018). *K–12 education: Discipline disparities for black students, boys, and students with disabilities*. Accessed at www.gao.gov/assets/700/690828.pdf on May 23, 2018.

van Beek, I., Taris, T. W., & Schaufeli, W. B. (2011). Workaholic and work engaged employees: Dead ringers or worlds apart? *Journal of Occupational Health Psychology, 16*(4), 468–482.

Waldner, L. S., McGorry, S. Y., & Widener, M. C. (2012). E-service-learning: The evolution of service-learning to engage a growing online student population. *Journal of Higher Education Outreach and Engagement, 16*(2), 123–150.

West, J. M., & Roberts, K. L. (2016). Caught up in curiosity: Genius hour in the kindergarten classroom. *Reading Teacher, 70*(2), 227–232.

West-Rosenthal, L. B. (2017, October 23). *9 key resources on trauma-informed schools* [Blog post]. Accessed at https://schoolleadersnow.weareteachers.com/9-resources-for-trauma-informed -school on October 16, 2018.

Wigfield, A., Guthrie, J. T., Perencevich, K. C., Taboada, A., Klauda, S. L., McRae, A., et al. (2008). Role of reading engagement in mediating effects of reading comprehension instruction on reading outcomes. *Psychology in the Schools, 45*(5), 432–445.

Wilson, V., & Jones, J. (2017). *This year's poverty data look a lot different when you break them down by race*. Accessed at https://talkpoverty.org/2017/09/13/years-poverty-data-look-lot-different -break-race on May 17, 2018.

Yazzie-Mintz, E. (2007). *Voices of students on engagement: A report on the 2006 High School Survey of Student Engagement*. Bloomington, IN: Center for Evaluation and Education Policy.

Young, M. I. (2017). *The effects of teaching reading using the gradual release of responsibility model and 4th grade reading*. Unpublished doctoral dissertation, Trevecca Nazarene University, Nashville, TN.

Zapata, Y. P., & Brooks, R. (2017). *Adapting unstoppable learning*. Bloomington, IN: Solution Tree Press.

Zyngier, D. (2011). (Re)conceptualising risk: Left numb and disengaged and lost in a no-man's-land or what (seems to) work for at-risk students. *International Journal of Inclusive Education, 15*(2), 211–231.

Index

Unstoppable Learning
Douglas Fisher and Nancy Frey
Discover proven methods to enhance teaching and learning schoolwide. Identify questions educators should ask to guarantee a positive classroom culture where students learn from each other, not just teachers. Explore ways to adapt teaching in response to students' individual needs.
BKF662

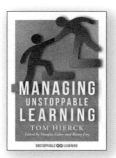

Managing Unstoppable Learning
Tom Hierck
Editors: Douglas Fisher and Nancy Frey
The Unstoppable Learning framework details seven essential elements of teaching and learning: planning, launching, consolidating, assessing, adapting, managing, and leading. This resource focuses specifically on the element of managing learning, outlining a collective approach to behavior management that minimizes negative behaviors and maximizes student potential.
BKF819

Adapting Unstoppable Learning
Yazmin Pineda Zapata and Rebecca Brooks
Editors: Douglas Fisher and Nancy Frey
This practical guide expands on the Unstoppable Learning model to explore accessible learning for students with varying needs, from physical disabilities to twice-exceptionality. Forms, tools, and diagrams designed to aid instructional planning are also included.
BKF734

A Handbook for Unstoppable Learning
Laurie Robinson Sammons and Nanci N. Smith
Editors: Douglas Fisher and Nancy Frey
Learn how to foster effective teaching and deep learning using the seven elements of the Unstoppable Learning model. Gain access to templates for planning learning targets, assessments, lessons, and units that will help create and maintain positive, healthy, high-performing classrooms.
BKF775

Wait! Your professional development journey doesn't have to end with the last pages of this book.

We realize improving student learning doesn't happen overnight. And your school or district shouldn't be left to puzzle out all the details of this process alone.

No matter where you are on the journey, we're committed to helping you get to the next stage.

Take advantage of everything from **custom workshops** to **keynote presentations** and **interactive web and video conferencing**. We can even help you develop an action plan tailored to fit your specific needs.

Let's get the conversation started.

Call 888.763.9045 today.

SolutionTree.com